AND EVEN NOW

MAX BEERBOHM

1st WORLD
LIBRARY
Literary Society

And Even Now

Max Beerbohm

© 1st World Library, 2006
PO Box 2211
Fairfield, IA 52556
www.1stworldlibrary.com
First Edition

LCCN: 2006936222

Softcover ISBN: 978-1-4218-3086-5
Hardcover ISBN: 978-1-4218-2986-9
eBook ISBN: 978-1-4218-3186-2

Purchase *"And Even Now"*
as a traditional bound book at:
www.1stWorldLibrary.com/purchase.asp?ISBN=978-1-4218-3086-5

1st World Library is a literary, educational organization dedicated to:

- Creating a free internet library of downloadable ebooks

- Hosting writing competitions and offering book publishing scholarships.

Interested in more 1st World Library books?
contact: literacy@1stworldlibrary.com
Check us out at: www.1stworldlibrary.com

1st World Library Literary Society

Giving Back to the World

"If you want to work on the core problem, it's early school literacy."

— James Barksdale, former CEO of Netscape

"No skill is more crucial to the future of a child, or to a democratic and prosperous society, than literacy."

— Los Angeles Times

Literacy... means far more than learning how to read and write... The aim is to transmit... knowledge and promote social participation."

— UNESCO

"Literacy is not a luxury, it is a right and a responsibility. If our world is to meet the challenges of the twenty-first century we must harness the energy and creativity of all our citizens."

— President Bill Clinton

"Parents should be encouraged to read to their children, and teachers should be equipped with all available techniques for teaching literacy, so the varying needs and capacities of individual kids can be taken into account."

— Hugh Mackay

TO MY WIFE

I offer here some of the essays that I have written in the course of the past ten years. While I was collecting them and (quite patiently) reading them again, I found that a few of them were in direct reference to the moments at which they were severally composed. It was clear that these must have their dates affixed to them. And for sake of uniformity I have dated all the others, and, doing so, have thought I need not exclude all such topical remarks as in them too were uttered, nor throw into a past tense such of those remarks as I have retained. Perhaps a book of essays ought to seem as if it had been written a few days before publication. On the other hand—but this is a Note, not a Preface.

M.B.
Rapallo, 1920.

CONTENTS

A RELIC (1918) 9
'HOW SHALL I WORD IT?' (1910) 16
MOBLED KING (1911) 25
KOLNIYATSCH (1913) 37
NO. 2. THE PINES (1914) 41
A LETTER THAT WAS NOT WRITTEN (1914) 61
BOOKS WITHIN BOOKS (1914) 66
THE GOLDEN DRUGGET (1918) 75
HOSTS AND GUESTS (1918) 80
A POINT TO BE REMEMBERED (1918) 93
SERVANTS (1918) 101
GOING OUT FOR A WALK (1918) 115
QUIA IMPERFECTUM (1918) 119
SOMETHING DEFEASIBLE (1919) 133
'A CLERGYMAN' (1918) 139
THE CRIME (1920) 145
IN HOMES UNBLEST (1919) 151
WILLIAM AND MARY (1920) 156
ON SPEAKING FRENCH (1919) 168
LAUGHTER (1920) 175

A RELIC

1918

Yesterday I found in a cupboard an old, small, battered portmanteau which, by the initials on it, I recognised as my own property. The lock appeared to have been forced. I dimly remembered having forced it myself, with a poker, in my hot youth, after some journey in which I had lost the key; and this act of violence was probably the reason why the trunk had so long ago ceased to travel. I unstrapped it, not without dust; it exhaled the faint scent of its long closure; it contained a tweed suit of Late Victorian pattern, some bills, some letters, a collar-stud, and—something which, after I had wondered for a moment or two what on earth it was, caused me suddenly to murmur, 'Down below, the sea rustled to and fro over the shingle.'

Strange that these words had, year after long year, been existing in some obscure cell at the back of my brain!—forgotten but all the while existing, like the trunk in that cupboard. What released them, what threw open the cell door, was nothing but the fragment of a fan; just the butt-end of an inexpensive fan. The sticks are of white bone, clipped together with a semicircular ring that is not silver. They are neatly oval at the base, but variously jagged at the other end. The longest of them measures perhaps two inches. Ring and all, they have no market value; for a farthing is the least coin in our currency. And yet, though I had so long forgotten them, for me they are not worthless. They touch a chord... Lest this confession raise false hopes in the reader, I add that I did not know their owner.

I did once see her, and in Normandy, and by moonlight, and her name was Ange'lique. She was graceful, she was even beautiful. I was but nineteen years old. Yet even so I cannot say that she impressed me favourably. I was seated at a table of a cafe' on the terrace of a casino. I sat facing the sea, with my back to the casino. I sat listening to the quiet sea, which I had crossed that morning. The hour was late, there were few people about. I heard the swing-door behind me flap open, and was aware of a sharp snapping and crackling sound as a lady in white passed quickly by me. I stared at her erect thin back and her agitated elbows. A short fat man passed in pursuit of her—an elderly man in a black alpaca jacket that billowed. I saw that she had left a trail of little white things on the asphalt. I watched the efforts of the agonised short fat man to overtake her as she swept wraith-like away to the distant end of the terrace. What was the matter? What had made her so spectacularly angry with him? The three or four waiters of the cafe' were exchanging cynical smiles and shrugs, as waiters will. I tried to feel cynical, but was thrilled with excitement, with wonder and curiosity. The woman out yonder had doubled on her tracks. She had not slackened her furious speed, but the man waddlingly contrived to keep pace with her now. With every moment they became more distinct, and the prospect that they would presently pass by me, back into the casino, gave me that physical tension which one feels on a wayside platform at the imminent passing of an express. In the rushingly enlarged vision I had of them, the wrath on the woman's face was even more saliently the main thing than I had supposed it would be. That very hard Parisian face must have been as white as the powder that coated it. '•coute, Ange'lique,' gasped the perspiring bourgeois, 'e'coute, je te supplie—' The swing- door received them and was left swinging to and fro. I wanted to follow, but had not paid for my bock. I beckoned my waiter. On his way to me he stooped down and picked up something which, with a smile and a shrug, he laid on my table: 'Il semble que Mademoiselle ne

10   Max Beerbohm

s'en servira plus.' This is the thing I now write of, and at sight of it I understood why there had been that snapping and crackling, and what the white fragments on the ground were.

I hurried through the rooms, hoping to see a continuation of that drama—a scene of appeasement, perhaps, or of fury still implacable. But the two oddly-assorted players were not performing there. My waiter had told me he had not seen either of them before. I suppose they had arrived that day. But I was not destined to see either of them again. They went away, I suppose, next morning; jointly or singly; singly, I imagine.

They made, however, a prolonged stay in my young memory, and would have done so even had I not had that tangible memento of them. Who were they, those two of whom that one strange glimpse had befallen me? What, I wondered, was the previous history of each? What, in particular, had all that tragic pother been about? Mlle. Ange'lique I guessed to be thirty years old, her friend perhaps fifty-five. Each of their faces was as clear to me as in the moment of actual vision—the man's fat shiny bewildered face; the taut white face of the woman, the hard red line of her mouth, the eyes that were not flashing, but positively dull, with rage. I presumed that the fan had been a present from him, and a recent present—bought perhaps that very day, after their arrival in the town. But what, what had he done that she should break it between her hands, scattering the splinters as who should sow dragon's teeth? I could not believe he had done anything much amiss. I imagined her grievance a trivial one. But this did not make the case less engrossing. Again and again I would take the fan-stump from my pocket, examining it on the palm of my hand, or between finger and thumb, hoping to read the mystery it had been mixed up in, so that I might reveal that mystery to the world. To the world, yes; nothing less than that. I was determined to make a story of what I had seen—a conte in the manner of great Guy de Maupassant. Now and again, in the course of the past year or so, it had occurred to me that I might be a writer. But I had not felt the impulse to sit down and write something. I did feel that impulse now. It would indeed have been an irresistible impulse if I had known just what to write.

I felt I might know at any moment, and had but to give my mind to it. Maupassant was an impeccable artist, but I think the secret of the hold he had on the young men of my day was not so much that we discerned his cunning as that we delighted in the simplicity which his cunning achieved. I had read a great number of his short stories, but none that had made me feel as though I, if I were a writer, mightn't have written it myself. Maupassant had an European reputation. It was pleasing, it was soothing and gratifying, to feel that one could at any time win an equal fame if one chose to set pen to paper. And now, suddenly, the spring had been touched in me, the time was come. I was grateful for the fluke by which I had witnessed on the terrace that evocative scene. I looked forward to reading the MS. of 'The Fan'—to-morrow, at latest. I was not wildly ambitious. I was not inordinately vain. I knew I couldn't ever, with the best will in the world, write like Mr. George Meredith. Those wondrous works of his, seething with wit, with poetry and philosophy and what not, never had beguiled me with the sense that I might do something similar. I had full consciousness of not being a philosopher, of not being a poet, and of not being a wit. Well, Maupassant was none of these things. He was just an observer, like me. Of course he was a good deal older than I, and had observed a good deal more. But it seemed to me that he was not my superior in knowledge of life. I knew all about life through him.

Dimly, the initial paragraph of my tale floated in my mind. I—not exactly I myself, but rather that impersonal je familiar to me through Maupassant—was to be sitting at that table, with a bock before me, just as I had sat. Four or five short sentences would give the whole scene. One of these I had quite definitely composed. You have already heard it. 'Down below, the sea rustled to and fro over the shingle.'

These words, which pleased me much, were to do double duty. They were to recur. They were to be, by a fine stroke, the very last words of my tale, their tranquillity striking a sharp ironic contrast with the stress of what had just been narrated. I had, you see, advanced further in the form of my tale than in the substance. But even the form was as yet vague. What, exactly, was to happen after Mlle. Ange'lique and M. Joumand (as I provisionally called him) had rushed back past me into the casino? It was clear that I must hear the whole inner history from the lips of one or the other of them. Which? Should M. Joumand stagger out on to the terrace, sit down heavily at the table next to mine, bury his head in his hands, and presently, in broken words, blurt out to me all that might be of interest?... "And I tell you I gave up everything for her—everything." He stared at me with his old hopeless eyes. "She is more than the fiend I have described to you. Yet I swear to you, monsieur, that if I had anything left to give, it should be hers."

'Down below, the sea rustled to and fro over the shingle.'

Or should the lady herself be my informant? For a while, I rather leaned to this alternative. It was more exciting, it seemed to make the writer more signally a man of the world. On the other hand, it was less simple to manage. Wronged persons might be ever so communicative, but I surmised that persons in the wrong were reticent. Mlle. Ange'lique, therefore, would have to be modified by me in appearance and behaviour, toned down, touched up; and poor M. Joumand must look like a man of whom one could believe anything.... 'She ceased speaking. She gazed down at the fragments of her fan, and then, as though finding in them an image of her own life, whispered, "To think what I once was, monsieur!—what, but for him, I might be, even now!" She buried her face in her hands, then stared out into the night. Suddenly she uttered a short, harsh laugh.

'Down below, the sea rustled to and fro over the shingle.'

I decided that I must choose the first of these two ways. It was the less chivalrous as well as the less lurid way, but clearly it was the more artistic as well as the easier. The 'chose vue,' the 'tranche de la vie'—this was the thing to aim at. Honesty was the best policy. I must be nothing if not merciless. Maupassant was nothing if not merciless. He would not have spared Mlle. Ange'lique. Besides, why should I libel M. Joumand? Poor—no, not poor M. Joumand! I warned myself against pitying him. One touch of 'sentimentality,' and I should be lost. M. Joumand was ridiculous. I must keep him so. But—what was his position in life? Was he a lawyer perhaps?—or the proprietor of a shop in the Rue de Rivoli? I toyed with the possibility that he kept a fan shop—that the business had once been a prosperous one, but had gone down, down, because of his infatuation for this woman to whom he was always giving fans—which she always smashed.... "Ah monsieur, cruel and ungrateful to me though she is, I swear to you that if I had anything left to give, it should be hers; but," he stared at me with his old hopeless eyes, "the fan she broke to-night was the last—the last, monsieur—of my stock." Down below,'-but I pulled myself together, and asked pardon of my Muse.

It may be that I had offended her by my fooling. Or it may be that she had a sisterly desire to shield Mlle. Ange'lique from my mordant art. Or it may be that she was bent on saving M. de Maupassant from a dangerous rivalry. Anyway, she withheld from me the inspiration I had so confidently solicited. I could not think what had led up to that scene on the terrace. I tried hard and soberly. I turned the 'chose vue' over and over in my mind, day by day, and the fan-stump over and over in my hand. But the 'chose a' figurer'—what, oh what, was that? Nightly I revisited the cafe', and sat there with an open mind—a mind wide-open to catch the idea that should drop into it like a ripe golden plum. The plum did not ripen. The mind remained wide-open for a week or more, but nothing except that phrase about the sea rustled to and fro in it.

A full quarter of a century has gone by. M. Joumand's death, so far too fat was he all those years ago, may be presumed. A temper so violent as Mlle. Ange'lique's must surely have brought its owner to the grave, long since. But here, all unchanged, the stump of her fan is; and once more I turn it over and over in my hand, not learning its secret—no, nor even trying to, now. The chord this relic strikes in me is not one of curiosity as to that old quarrel, but (if you will forgive me) one of tenderness for my first effort to write, and for my first hopes of excellence.

'HOW SHALL I WORD IT?'

1910

It would seem that I am one of those travellers for whom the railway bookstall does not cater. Whenever I start on a journey, I find that my choice lies between well-printed books which I have no wish to read, and well-written books which I could not read without permanent injury to my eyesight. The keeper of the bookstall, seeing me gaze vaguely along his shelves, suggests that I should take 'Fen Country Fanny' or else 'The Track of Blood' and have done with it. Not wishing to hurt his feelings, I refuse these works on the plea that I have read them. Whereon he, divining despite me that I am a superior person, says 'Here is a nice little handy edition of More's "Utopia"' or 'Carlyle's "French Revolution"' and again I make some excuse. What pleasure could I get from trying to cope with a masterpiece printed in diminutive grey-ish type on a semi-transparent little grey-ish page? I relieve the bookstall of nothing but a newspaper or two.

The other day, however, my eye and fancy were caught by a book entitled 'How Shall I Word It?' and sub-entitled 'A Complete Letter Writer for Men and Women.' I had never read one of these manuals, but had often heard that there was a great and constant 'demand' for them. So I demanded this one. It is no great fun in itself. The writer is no fool. He has evidently a natural talent for writing letters. His style is, for the most part, discreet and easy. If you were a young man writing 'to Father of Girl he wishes to Marry' or 'thanking Fiance'e for

Present' or 'reproaching Fiancé'e for being a Flirt,' or if you were a mother 'asking Governess her Qualifications' or 'replying to Undesirable Invitation for her Child,' or indeed if you were in any other one of the crises which this book is designed to alleviate, you might copy out and post the specially-provided letter without making yourself ridiculous in the eyes of its receiver—unless, of course, he or she also possessed a copy of the book. But—well, can you conceive any one copying out and posting one of these letters, or even taking it as the basis for composition? You cannot. That shows how little you know of your fellow-creatures. Not you nor I can plumb the abyss at the bottom of which such humility is possible. Nevertheless, as we know by that great and constant 'demand,' there the abyss is, and there multitudes are at the bottom of it. Let's peer down... No, all is darkness. But faintly, if we listen hard, is borne up to us a sound of the scratching of innumerable pens—pens whose wielders are all trying, as the author of this handbook urges them, to 'be original, fresh, and interesting' by dint of more or less strict adherence to sample.

Giddily you draw back from the edge of the abyss. Come!—here is a thought to steady you. The mysterious great masses of helpless folk for whom 'How Shall I Word It' is written are sound at heart, delicate in feeling, anxious to please, most loth to wound. For it must be presumed that the author's style of letter-writing is informed as much by a desire to give his public what it needs, and will pay for, as by his own beautiful nature; and in the course of all the letters that he dictates you will find not one harsh word, not one ignoble thought or unkind insinuation. In all of them, though so many are for the use of persons placed in the most trying circumstances, and some of them are for persons writhing under a sense of intolerable injury, sweetness and light do ever reign. Even 'yours truly, Jacob Langton,' in his 'letter to his Daughter's Mercenary Fiancé',' mitigates the sternness of his tone by the remark that his 'task is inexpressibly painful.' And he, Mr. Langton, is the one writer who lets the post go out on his wrath. When Horace Masterton, of Thorpe Road, Putney, receives from Miss Jessica Weir, of Fir Villa, Blackheath, a letter 'declaring her Change of Feelings,' does he upbraid her? No; 'it was honest and brave of you to write to me so straightforwardly and at the back of my mind I know you have done what is best.... I give you back your freedom only at your desire. God bless you, dear.' Not less admirable is the behaviour, in similar case, of Cecil Grant (14, Glover Street, Streatham). Suddenly, as a bolt from the blue, comes a letter from Miss Louie Hawke (Elm View, Deerhurst), breaking off her betrothal to him. Haggard, he sits down to his desk; his pen traverses the notepaper—calling down curses on Louie and on all her sex? No; 'one cannot say good-bye for ever without deep regret to days that have been so full of happiness. I must thank you sincerely for all your great kindness to me.... With every sincere wish for your future happiness,' he bestows complete freedom on Miss Hawke. And do not imagine that in the matter of self-control and sympathy, of power to understand all and pardon all, the men are lagged behind by the women. Miss Leila Johnson (The Manse, Carlyle) has observed in Leonard Wace (Dover Street, Saltburn) a certain coldness of demeanour; yet 'I do not blame you; it is probably your nature'; and Leila in her sweet forbearance is typical of all the other pained women in these pages: she is but one of a crowd of heroines.

Face to face with all this perfection, the not perfect reader begins to crave some little outburst of wrath, of hatred or malice, from one of these imaginary ladies and gentlemen. He longs for—how shall he word it?—a glimpse of some bad motive, of some little lapse from dignity. Often, passing by a pillar-box, I have wished I could unlock it and carry away its contents, to be studied at my leisure. I have always thought such a haul would abound in things fascinating to a student of human nature. One night, not long ago, I took a waxen impression of the lock of the pillar-box nearest to my house, and had a key made. This implement I have as yet lacked either the courage or the opportunity to use. And now I think I shall throw it away.... No, I shan't. I refuse, after all, to draw my inference that the bulk of the British public writes always in the manner of this handbook. Even if they all have beautiful natures they must sometimes be sent slightly astray by inferior impulses, just as are you and I.

And, if err they must, surely it were well they should know how to do it correctly and forcibly. I suggest to our author that he should sprinkle his next edition with a few less righteous examples, thereby both purging his book of its monotony and somewhat justifying its sub-title. Like most people who are in the habit of writing things to be printed, I have not the knack of writing really good letters. But let me crudely indicate the sort of thing that our manual needs....

LETTER FROM POOR MAN TO OBTAIN MONEY FROM RICH ONE.

[The English law is particularly hard on what is called blackmail. It is therefore essential that the applicant should write nothing that might afterwards be twisted to incriminate him.—ED.]

DEAR SIR,

To-day, as I was turning out a drawer in my attic, I came across a letter which by a curious chance fell into my hands some years ago, and which, in the stress of grave pecuniary embarrassment, had escaped my memory. It is a letter written by yourself to a lady, and the date shows it to have been written shortly after your marriage. It is of a confidential nature, and might, I fear, if it fell into the wrong hands, be cruelly misconstrued. I would wish you to have the satisfaction of destroying it in person. At first I thought of sending it on to you by post. But I know how happy you are in your domestic life; and probably your wife and you, in your perfect mutual trust, are in the habit of opening each other's letters. Therefore, to avoid risk, I would prefer to hand the document to you personally. I will not ask you to come to my attic, where I could not offer you such hospitality as is due to a man of your wealth and position. You will be so good as to meet me at 3.0 A.M. (sharp) to-morrow (Thursday) beside the tenth lamp-post to the left on the Surrey side of Waterloo Bridge; at which hour and place we shall not be disturbed. I am, dear Sir,

Yours respectfully,

JAMES GRIDGE.

LETTER FROM YOUNG MAN REFUSING TO PAY HIS TAILOR'S BILL.

Mr. Eustace Davenant has received the half-servile, half-insolent screed which Mr. Yardley has addressed to him. Let Mr. Yardley cease from crawling on his knees and shaking his fist. Neither this posture nor this gesture can wring one bent farthing from the pockets of Mr. Davenant, who was a minor at the time when that series of ill-made suits was supplied to him and will hereafter, as in the past, shout (without prejudice) from the house-tops that of all the tailors in London Mr. Yardley is at once the most grasping and the least competent.

LETTER TO THANK AUTHOR FOR INSCRIBED COPY OF BOOK.

DEAR MR. EMANUEL FLOWER,

It was kind of you to think of sending me a copy of your new book. It would have been kinder still to think again and abandon that project. I am a man of gentle instincts, and do not like to tell you that 'A Flight into Arcady' (of which I have skimmed a few pages, thus wasting two or three minutes of my not altogether worthless time) is trash. On the other hand, I am determined that you shall not be able to go around boasting to your friends, if you have any, that this work was not condemned, derided, and dismissed by your sincere well-wisher,

WREXFORD CRIPPS.

LETTER TO MEMBER OF PARLIAMENT UNSEATED AT GENERAL ELECTION.

DEAR MR. POBSBY-BURFORD,

Though I am myself an ardent Tory, I cannot but rejoice in the crushing defeat you have just suffered in West Odgetown. There are moments when political conviction is overborne by personal sentiment; and this is one of them. Your loss of the seat that you held is the more striking by reason of the splendid manner in which the northern and eastern divisions of Odgetown have been wrested from the Liberal Party. The great bulk of the newspaper-reading public will be puzzled by your extinction in the midst of our party's triumph. But then, the great mass of the newspaper-reading public has not met you. I have. You will probably not remember me. You are the sort of man who would not remember anybody who might not be of some definite use to him. Such, at least, was one of the impressions you made on me when I met you last summer at a dinner given by our friends the Pelhams. Among the other things in you that struck me were the blatant pomposity of your manner, your appalling flow of cheap platitudes, and your hoggish lack of ideas. It is such men as you that lower the tone of public life. And I am sure that in writing to you thus I am but expressing what is felt, without distinction of party, by all who sat with you in the late Parliament.

The one person in whose behalf I regret your withdrawal into private life is your wife, whom I had the pleasure of taking in to the aforesaid dinner. It was evident to me that she was a woman whose spirit was well-nigh broken by her conjunction with you. Such remnants of cheerfulness as were in her I attributed to the Parliamentary duties which kept you out of her sight for so very many hours daily. I do not like to think of the fate to which the free and independent electors of West Odgetown have just condemned her. Only, remember this: chattel of yours though she is, and timid and humble, she despises you in her heart. I am, dear Mr. Pobsby-Burford,

Yours very truly,

HAROLD THISTLAKE.

LETTER FROM YOUNG LADY IN ANSWER TO INVITATION FROM OLD SCHOOLMISTRESS.

MY DEAR MISS PRICE,

How awfully sweet of you to ask me to stay with you for a few days but how can you think I may have forgotten you for of course I think of you so very often and of the three ears I spent at your school because it is such a joy not to be there any longer and if one is at all down it bucks one up derectly to remember that thats all over atanyrate and that one has enough food to nurrish one and not that awful monottany of life and not the petty fogging daily tirrany you went in for and I can imagin no greater thrill and luxury in a way than to come and see the whole dismal grind still going on but without me being in it but this would be rather beastly of me wouldnt it so please dear Miss Price dont expect me and do excuse mistakes of English Composition and Spelling and etcetra in your affectionate old pupil,

EMILY TH•RESE LYNN-ROYSTON.

ps, I often rite to people telling them where I was edducated and highly reckomending you.

LETTER IN ACKNOWLEDGEMENT OF WEDDING PRESENT.

DEAR LADY AMBLESHAM,

Who gives quickly, says the old proverb, gives twice. For this reason I have purposely delayed writing to you, lest I should appear to thank you more than once for the small, cheap, hideous present you sent me on the occasion of my recent wedding. Were you a poor woman, that little bowl of ill-imitated Dresden china would convict you of tastelessness merely; were you a blind woman, of nothing but an odious parsimony. As you have normal eyesight and more than normal wealth, your gift to me proclaims you at once a Philistine and a miser (or rather did so proclaim you until, less than ten seconds after I had unpacked it from its wrappings of tissue paper, I took it to the open window and had the satisfaction of seeing it shattered to atoms on the pavement). But stay! I perceive a possible flaw in my argument. Perhaps you were guided in your choice by a definite wish to insult me. I am sure, on reflection, that this was so. I shall not forget.

Yours, etc.,

CYNTHIA BEAUMARSH.

PS. My husband asks me to tell you to warn Lord Amblesham to keep out of his way or to assume some disguise so complete that he will not be recognised by him and horsewhipped.

PPS. I am sending copies of this letter to the principal London and provincial newspapers.

LETTER FROM...

But enough! I never thought I should be so strong in this line. I had not foreseen such copiousness and fatal fluency. Never again will I tap these deep dark reservoirs in a character that had always seemed to me, on the whole, so amiable.

MOBLED KING

1911

Just as a memorial, just to perpetuate in one's mind the dead man in whose image and honour it has been erected, this statue is better than any that I have seen.... No, pedantic reader: I ought not to have said 'than any other that I have seen' Except in shrouded and distorted outline, I have not seen this statue.

Not as an image, then, can it be extolled by me. And I am bound to say that even as an honour it seems to me more than dubious. Commissioned and designed and chiselled and set up in all reverence, it yet serves very well the purpose of a guy. This does not surprise you. You are familiar with a host of statues that are open to precisely that objection. Westminster Abbey abounds in them. They confront you throughout London and the provinces. They stud the Continent. Rare indeed is the statue that can please the well-wishers of the person portrayed. Nor in every case is the sculptor to blame. There is in the art of sculpture itself a quality intractable to the aims of personal portraiture. Sculpture, just as it cannot fitly record the gesture of a moment, is discommoded by personal idiosyncrasies. The details that go to compose this or that gentleman's appearance—such as the little wrinkles around his eyes, and the way his hair grows, and the special convolutions of his ears—all these, presentable on canvas, or evocable by words, are not right matter for the chisel or for the mould and furnace. Translated into terms of bronze or marble, howsoever cunningly, these slight and trivial things cease to be trivial and slight. They assume a ludicrous importance. No man is worthy to be reproduced as bust or statue. And if sculpture is too august to deal with what a man has received from his Maker, how much less ought it to be bothered about what he has received from his hosier and tailor! Sculpture's province is the soul. The most concrete, it is also the most spiritual of the arts. The very heaviness and stubbornness of its material, precluding it from happy dalliance with us fleeting individual creatures, fit it to cope with that which in mankind is permanent and universal. It can through the symbol give us incomparably the type. Wise is that sculptor who, when portray an individual he must, treats arbitrarily the mere actual husk, and strives but to show the soul. Of course, he must first catch that soul. What M. Rodin knew about the character and career of Mr. George Wyndham, or about the character and career of Mr. Bernard Shaw, was not, I hazard, worth knowing; and Mr. Shaw is handed down by him to posterity as a sort of bearded lady, and Mr. Wyndham as a sort of beardless one. But about Honore' de Balzac he knew much. Balzac he understood. Balzac's work, Balzac's soul, in that great rugged figure aspiring and indeflexible, he gave us with a finality that could have been achieved through no other art than sculpture.

There is a close kinship between that statue of Balzac and this statue of which I am to tell you. Both induce, above all, a profound sense of unrest, of heroic will to overcome all obstacles. The will to compass self-expression, the will to emerge from darkness to light, from formlessness to form, from nothing to everything—this it is that I find in either statue; and this it is in virtue of which the Balzac has unbeknown a brother on the Italian seaboard.

Here stands—or rather struggles—on his pedestal this younger brother, in strange contrast with the scenery about him. Mildly, behind his back, the sea laps the shingle. Mildly, in front of him, on the other side of the road, rise some of those mountains whereby the Earth, before she settled down to cool, compassed—she, too—some sort of self-expression. Mildly around his pedestal, among rusty anchors strewn there on the grass between road and beach, sit the fishermen, mending their nets or their sails, or whittling bits of wood. What will you say of these fishermen when—but I outstrip my narrative.

I had no inkling of tragedy when first I came to the statue. I did not even know it was a statue. I had made by night the short journey from Genoa to this place beside the sea; and, driving along the coast-road to the hotel that had been recommended, I passed what in the starlight looked like nothing but an elderly woman mounted on a square pedestal and gazing out seaward—a stout, elderly, lonely woman in a poke bonnet, indescribable except by that old Victorian term 'a party,' and as unlike Balzac's younger brother as only Sarah Gamp's elder sister could be. How, I wondered in my hotel, came the elder sister of Sarah Gamp to be here in Liguria and in the twentieth century? How clomb she, puffing and panting, on to that pedestal? For what argosy of gin was she straining her old eyes seaward? I knew there would be no sleep for me until I had solved these problems; and I went forth afoot along the way I had come. The moon had risen; and presently I saw in the starlight the 'party' who so intrigued me. Eminent, amorphous, mysterious, there she stood, immobile, voluminous, ghastly beneath the moon. By a slight shoreward lift of crinoline, as against the seaward protrusion of poke bonnet, a grotesque balance was given to the unshapely shape of her. For all her uncanniness, I thought I had never seen any one, male or female, old or young, look so hopelessly common. I felt that by daylight a noble vulgarity might be hers. In the watches of the night she was hopelessly, she was transcendently common.

Little by little, as I came nearer, she ceased to illude me, and I began to think of her as 'it.' What 'it' was, however, I knew not until I was at quite close quarters to the pedestal it rose from. There, on the polished granite, was carved this legend:

A UMBERTO Iø

And instinctively, as my eye travelled up, my hand leapt to the salute; for I stood before the veiled image of a dead king, and had been guilty of a misconception that dishonoured him.

Standing respectfully at one angle and another, I was able to form, by the outlines of the grey sheeting that enveloped him, some rough notion of his posture and his costume. Round what was evidently his neck the sheeting was constricted by ropes; and the height and girth of the bundle above—to half-closed eyes, even now, an averted poke-bonnet—gave token of a tall helmet with a luxuriant shock of plumes waving out behind. Immediately beneath the ropes, the breadth and sharpness of the bundle hinted at epaulettes. And the protrusion that had seemed to be that of a wind-blown crinoline was caused, I thought, by the king having his left hand thrust well out to grasp the hilt of his inclined sword. Altogether, I had soon builded a clear enough idea of his aspect; and I promised myself a curious gratification in comparing anon this idea with his aspect as it really was.

Yes, I took it for granted that the expectant statue was to be unveiled within the next few days. I was glad to be in time—not knowing in how terribly good time I was—for the ceremony. Not since my early childhood had I seen the unveiling of a statue; and on that occasion I had struck a discordant note by weeping bitterly. I dare say you know that statue of William Harvey which stands on the Leas at Folkestone. You say you were present at the unveiling? Well, I was the child who cried. I had been told that William Harvey was a great and good man who discovered the circulation of the blood; and my mind had leapt, in all the swiftness of its immaturity, to the conclusion that his statue would be a bright blood-red. Cruel was the thrill of dismay I had when at length the cord was pulled and the sheeting slid down, revealing so dull a sight…

Contemplating the veiled Umberto, I remembered that sight, remembered those tears unworthy (as my nurse told me) of a little gentleman. Years had passed. I was grown older and wiser. I had learnt to expect less of life. There was no fear that I should disgrace myself in the matter of Umberto.

I was not so old, though, nor so wise, as I am now. I expected more than there is of Italian speed, and less than there is of Italian subtlety. A whole year has passed since first I set eyes on veiled Umberto. And Umberto is still veiled.

And veiled for more than a whole year, as I now know, had Umberto been before my coming. Four years before that, the municipal council, it seems, had voted the money for him. His father, of sensational memory, was here already, in the middle of the main piazza, of course. And Garibaldi was hard by; so was Mazzini; so was Cavour. Umberto was still implicit in a block of marble, high upon one of the mountains of Carrara. The task of educing him was given to a promising young sculptor who lived here. Down came the block of marble, and was transported to the studio of the promising young sculptor; and out, briskly enough, mustachios and all, came Umberto. He looked very regal, I am sure, as he stood glaring around with his prominent marble eyeballs, and snuffing the good fresh air of the world as far as might be into shallow marble nostrils. He looked very authoritative and fierce and solemn, I am sure. He made, anyhow, a deep impression on the mayor and councillors, and the only question was as to just where he should be erected. The granite pedestal had already been hewn and graven; but a worthy site was to seek. Outside the railway station? He would obstruct the cabs. In the Giardino Pubblico? He would clash with Garibaldi. Every councillor had a pet site, and every other one a pet objection to it. That strip of waste ground where the fishermen sat pottering? It was too humble, too far from the centre of things. Meanwhile, Umberto stayed in the studio. Dust settled on his epaulettes. A year went by. Spiders ventured to spin their webs from his plumes to his mustachios. Another year went by. Whenever the councillors had nothing else to talk about they talked about the site for Umberto.

Presently they became aware that among the poorer classes of the town had arisen a certain hostility to the statue. The councillors suspected that the priesthood had been at work. The forces of reaction against the forces of progress! Very well! The councillors hurriedly decided that the best available site, on the whole, was that strip of waste ground where the fishermen sat pottering. The pedestal was promptly planted. Umberto was promptly wrapped up, put on a lorry, wheeled to the place, and hoisted into position. The date of the unveiling was fixed. The mayor I am told, had already composed his speech, and was getting it by heart. Around the pedestal the fishermen sat pottering. It was not observed that they received any visits from the priests.

But priests are subtle; and it is a fact that three days before the date of the unveiling the fishermen went, all in their black Sunday clothes, and claimed audience of the mayor. He laid aside the MS. of his speech, and received them affably. Old Agostino, their spokesman, he whose face is so marvellously wrinkled, lifted his quavering voice. He told the mayor, with great respect, that the rights of the fishermen had been violated. That piece of ground had for hundreds of years belonged to them. They had not been consulted about that statue. They did not want it there. It was in the way, and must (said Agostino) be removed. At first the mayor was inclined to treat the deputation with a light good humour, and to resume the study of his MS. But Agostino had a MS. of his own. This was a copy of a charter whereby, before mayors and councillors were, the right to that piece of land had been granted in perpetuity to the fisherfolk of the district. The mayor, not committing himself to any opinion of the validity of the document, said that he—but there, it is tedious to report the speeches of mayors. Agostino told his mayor that a certain great lawyer would be arriving from Genoa to-morrow. It were tedious to report what passed between that great lawyer and the mayor and councillors assembled. Suffice it that the councillors were frightened, the date of the unveiling was postponed, and the whole matter, referred to high authorities in Rome, went darkly drifting into some form of litigation, and there abides.

Technically, then, neither side may claim that it has won. The statue has not been unveiled. But the statue has not been displaced. Practically, though, and morally, the palm is, so far, to the fishermen. The pedestal does not really irk them at all. On the contrary, it and the sheeting do cast for them in the heat a pleasant shadow, of which (the influence of Fleet Street, once felt, never shaken off, forces me to say) they are not slow to avail themselves. And the cost of the litigation comes not, you may be sure, out of their light old pockets, but out of the coffers of some pious rich folk hereabouts. The Pope remains a prisoner in the Vatican? Well, here is Umberto, a kind of hostage. Yet with what a difference! Here is no spiritual king stripped of earthly kingship. Here is an earthly king kept swaddled up day after day, to be publicly ridiculous. The fishermen, as I have said, pay him no heed. The mayor, passing along the road, looks straight in front of him, with an elaborate assumption of unconcern. So do the councillors. But there are others who look maliciously up at the hapless figure. Now and again there comes a monk from the monastery on that hill yonder. He laughs into his beard as he goes by. Two by two, in their grey cloaks and their blue mantillas, the little orphan girls are sometimes marched past. There they go, as I write. Not malice, but a vague horror, is in the eyes they turn. Umberto, belike, is used as a means to frighten them when, or lest, they offend. The nun in whose charge they are crosses herself.

Yet it is recorded of Umberto that he was kind to little children. This, indeed, is one of the few things recorded of him. Fierce though he looked, he was, for the most part, it must be confessed, null. He seldom asserted himself. There was so little of that for him to assert. He had, therefore, no personal enemies. In a negative way, he was popular, and was positively popular, for a while, after his assassination. And this it is that makes him now the less able, poor fellow, to understand and endure the shame he is put to. 'Stat rex indignatus.' He does try to assert himself now—does strive, by day and by night, poor petrefact, to rip off these fell and clownish integuments. Of his elder brother in Paris he has never heard; but he knows that Lazarus arisen from the tomb did not live in grave-clothes. He forgets that after all he is only a statue. To himself he is still a king—or at least a man who was once a king and, having done no wrong, ought not now to be insulted. If he had in his composition one marble grain of humour, he might... but no, a joke against oneself is always cryptic. Fat men are not always the best drivers of fat oxen; and cryptic statues cannot be depended on to see cryptic jokes.

If Umberto could grasp the truth that no man is worthy to be reproduced as a statue; if he could understand, once and for all, that the unveiling of him were itself a notable disservice to him, then might his wrath be turned to acquiescence, and his acquiescence to gratitude, and he be quite happy hid. Is he, really, more ridiculous now than he always was? If you be an extraordinary man, as was his father, win a throne by all means: you will fill it. If your son be another extraordinary man, he will fill it when his turn comes. But if that son be, as, alas, he most probably will be, like Umberto, quite ordinary, then let parental love triumph over pride of dynasty: advise your boy to abdicate at the earliest possible moment. A great king—what better? But it is ill that a throne be sat on by one whose legs dangle uncertainly towards the dai"s, and ill that a crown settle down over the tip of the nose. And the very fact that for quite inadequate kings men's hands do leap to the salute, instinctively, does but make us, on reflection, the more conscious of the whole absurdity. Even than a great man on a throne we can, when we reflect, imagine something—ah, not something better perhaps, but something more remote from absurdity. Let us say that Umberto's father was great, as well as extraordinary. He was accounted great enough to be the incarnation of a great idea. 'United Italy'—oh yes, a great idea, a charming idea: in the 'sixties I should have been all for it. But how shall I or any other impartial person write odes to the reality? What people in all this exquisite peninsula are to-day the happier for the things done by and through Vittorio Emmanuele Liberator?

The question is not merely rhetorical. There is the large class of politicians, who would have had no scope in the old days. And there are the many men who in other days would have been fishing or ploughing, but now strut in this and that official uniform. There passes between me and the sea, as I write—how opportunely people do pass here!—a little man with a peaked cap and light blue breeches and a sword. His prime duty is to see that none of his fellow peasants shall carry home a bucket of sea-water. For there is salt in sea-water; and heavily, because they must have it or sicken, salt is taxed; and this passing sentinel is to prevent them from cheating the Revenue by recourse to the sea which, though here it is, they must not regard as theirs. What becomes of the tax-money? It goes towards the building of battleships, cruisers, gunboats and so forth. What are these for? Why, for Italy to be a Great European Power with, of course. In the little blue bay behind Umberto, while I write, there lies at anchor an Italian gunboat. Opportunely again? I can but assure you that it really and truly is there. It has been there for two days. It delights the fishermen. They say it is 'bella e pulita com' un fiore.' They stand shading their eyes towards it, smiling and proud, heirs of all the ages, neglecting their sails and nets and spars of wood. They can imagine nothing better than it. They see nothing at all sinister or absurd about it, these simple fellows. And simple Umberto, their captive, strives to wheel round on his pedestal and to tear but a peep-hole in his sheeting. He would be glad could he feast but one eye on this bit of national glory. But he remains helpless—helpless as a Sultana made ready for the Bosphorus, helpless as a pig is in a poke. It enrages him that he who was so eminently respectable in life should be made so ludicrous on his eminence after death. He is bitter at the inertia of the men who set him up. Were he an ornament of the Church, not of the State that he served so conscientiously, how very different would be the treatment of his plight! If he were a Saint, occluded thus by the municipality, how many the prayers that would be muttered, the candles promised, for his release! There would be processions, too; and who knows but that there might even be a miracle vouchsafed, a rending of the veil? The only procession that passes him is that of the intimidated orphans. No heavenly power intervenes for him—perhaps (he bitterly conjectures) for fear of offending the Vatican. Sirocco, now and again, blows furiously at his back, but never splits the sheeting. Rain often soaks it, never rots it. There is no help for him. He stands a mock to the pious, a shame and incubus to the emancipated; received, yet hushed up; exalted, yet made a fool of; taken and left; a monument to Fate's malice.

From under the hem of his weather-beaten domino, always, he just displays, with a sort of tragic coquetry, the toe of a stout and serviceable marble boot. And this, I have begun to believe, is all that I shall ever see of him. Else might I not be writing about him; for else had he not so haunted me. If I knew myself destined to see him—to see him steadily and see him whole—no matter how many years hence, I could forthwith think about other things. I had hoped that by this essay I might rid my mind of him. He is inexcutible, confound him! His pedestal draws me to itself with some such fascination as had the altar of the unknown god for the wondering Greek. I try to distract myself by thinking of other images—images that I have seen. I think of Bartolommeo Colleoni riding greatly forth under the shadow of the church of Saint John and Saint Paul. Of Mr. Peabody I think, cosy in his armchair behind the Royal Exchange; of Nelson above the sparrows, and of Perseus among the pigeons; of golden Albert, and of Harvey the not red. Up looms Umberto, uncouthly casting them one and all into the shade. I think of other statues that I have not seen—statues suspected of holding something back from even the clearest-eyed men who have stood beholding and soliciting them. But how obvious, beside Umberto, the Sphinx would be! And Memnon, how tamely he sits waiting for the dawn!

Matchless as a memorial, then, I say again, this statue is. And as a work of art it has at least the advantage of being beyond criticism. In my young days, I wrote a plea that all the statues in the streets and squares of London should be extirpated and, according to their materials, smashed or melted. From an aesthetic standpoint, I went a trifle too far: London has a few good statues. From an humane standpoint, my plea was all wrong. Let no violence be done to the effigies of the dead. There is disrespect in setting up a dead man's effigy and then not unveiling it . But there would be no disrespect, and there would be no violence, if the bad statues familiar to London were ceremoniously veiled, and their inscribed pedestals left just as they are. That is a scheme which occurred to me soon after I saw the veiled Umberto. Mr. Birrell has now stepped in and forestalled my advocacy. Pereant qui—but no, who could wish that charming man to perish? The realisation of that scheme is what matters.

Let an inventory be taken of those statues. Let it be submitted to Lord Rosebery, and he be asked to tick off all those statesmen, poets, philosophers and other personages about whom he would wish to orate. Then let the list be passed on to other orators, until every statue on it shall have its particular spokesman. Then let the dates for the various veilings be appointed. If there be four or five veilings every week, I conceive that the whole list will be exhausted in two years or so. And my enjoyment of the reported speeches will not be the less keen because I can so well imagine them.... In conclusion, Lord Rosebery said that the keynote to the character of the man in whose honour they were gathered together to-day was, first and last, integrity. (Applause.) He did not say of him that he had been infallible. Which of us was infallible? (Laughter.) But this he would say, that the great man whose statue they were looking on for the last time had been actuated throughout his career by no motive but the desire to do that, and that only, which would conduce to the honour and to the stability of the country that gave him birth. Of him it might truly be said, as had been said of another, 'That which he had to give, he gave.' (Loud and prolonged applause.) His Lordship then pulled the cord, and the sheeting rolled up into position...

Not, however, because those speeches will so edify and soothe me, nor merely because those veiled statues will make less uncouth the city I was born in, do I feverishly thrust on you my proposition. The wish in me is that posterity shall be haunted by our dead heroes even as I am by Umberto. Rather hard on posterity? Well, the prevision of its plight would cheer me in mine immensely.

KOLNIYATSCH

1913

None of us who keep an eye on the heavens of European literature can forget the emotion that we felt when, but a few years since, the red star of Kolniyatsch swam into our ken. As nobody can prove that I wasn't, I claim now that I was the first to gauge the magnitude of this star and to predict the ascendant course which it has in fact triumphantly taken. That was in the days when Kolniyatsch was still alive. His recent death gives the cue for the boom. Out of that boom I, for one, will not be left. I rush to scrawl my name, large, on the tombstone of Kolniyatsch.

These foreign fellows always are especially to be commended. By the mere mention of their names you evoke in reader or hearer a vague sense of your superiority and his. Thank heaven, we are no longer insular. I don't say we have no native talent. We have heaps of it, pyramids of it, all around. But where, for the genuine thrill, would England be but for her good fortune in being able to draw on a seemingly inexhaustible supply of anguished souls from the Continent—infantile wide-eyed Slavs, Titan Teutons, greatly blighted Scandinavians, all of them different, but all of them raving in one common darkness and with one common gesture plucking out their vitals for exportation? There is no doubt that our continuous receipt of this commodity has had a bracing effect on our national character. We used to be rather phlegmatic, used we not? We have learnt to be vibrant.

Of Kolniyatsch, as of all authentic master-spirits in literature, it is true that he must be judged rather by what he wrote than by what he was. But the quality of his genius, albeit nothing if not national and also universal, is at the same time so deeply personal that we cannot afford to close our eyes on his life—a life happily not void of those sensational details which are what we all really care about.

'If you have tears, prepare to shed them now.' Kolniyatsch was born, last of a long line of rag-pickers, in 1886. At the age of nine he had already acquired that passionate alcoholism which was to have so great an influence in the moulding of his character and on the trend of his thought. Otherwise he does not seem to have shown in childhood any exceptional promise. It was not before his eighteenth birthday that he murdered his grandmother and was sent to that asylum in which he wrote the poems and plays belonging to what we now call his earlier manner. In 1907 he escaped from his sanctum, or chuzketc (cell) as he sardonically called it, and, having acquired some money by an act of violence, gave, by sailing for America, early proof that his genius was of the kind that crosses frontiers and seas. Unfortunately, it was not of the kind that passes Ellis Island. America, to her lasting shame, turned him back. Early in 1908 we find him once more in his old quarters, working at those novels and confessions on which, in the opinion of some, his fame will ultimately rest. Alas, we don't find him there now. It will be a fortnight ago to-morrow that Luntic Kolniyatsch passed peacefully away, in the twenty-eighth year of his age. He would have been the last to wish us to indulge in any sickly sentimentality. 'Nothing is here for tears, nothing but well and fair, and what may quiet us in a death so noble.'

Was Kolniyatsch mad? It depends on what we mean by that word. If we mean, as the bureaucrats of Ellis Island and, to their lasting shame, his friends and relations presumably meant, that he did not share our own smug and timid philosophy of life, then indeed was Kolniyatsch not sane. Granting for sake of argument that he was mad in a wider sense than that, we do but oppose an insuperable stumbling-block to the Eugenists. Imagine what Europe would be to-day, had Kolniyatsch not been! As one of the critics avers, 'It is hardly too much to say that a time may be not far distant, and may indeed be nearer than many of us suppose, when Luntic Kolniyatsch will, rightly or wrongly, be reckoned by some of us as not the least of those writers who are especially symptomatic of the early twentieth century and are possibly "for all time" or for a more or less certainly not inconsiderable period of time.' That is finely said. But I myself go somewhat further. I say that Kolniyatsch's message has drowned all previous messages and will drown any that may be uttered in the remotest future. You ask me what, precisely, that message was? Well, it is too elemental, too near to the very heart of naked Nature, for exact definition. Can you describe the message of an angry python more satisfactorily than as S-s-s-s? Or that of an infuriated bull better than as Moo? That of Kolniyatsch lies somewhere between these two. Indeed, at whatever point we take him, we find him hard to fit into any single category. Was he a realist or a romantic? He was neither, and he was both. By more than one critic he has been called a pessimist, and it is true that a part of his achievement may be gauged by the lengths to which he carried pessimism—railing and raging, not, in the manner of his tame forerunners, merely at things in general, or at women, or at himself, but lavishing an equally fierce scorn and hatred on children, on trees and flowers and the moon, and indeed on everything that the sentimentalists have endeavoured to force into favour. On the other hand, his burning faith in a personal Devil, his frank delight in earthquakes and pestilences, and his belief that every one but himself will be brought back to life in time to be frozen to death in the next glacial epoch, seem rather to stamp him as an optimist. By birth and training a man of the people, he was yet an aristocrat to the finger-tips, and Byron would have called him brother, though one trembles to think what he would have called Byron. First and last, he was an artist, and it is by reason of his technical mastery that he most of all outstands. Whether in prose or in verse, he compasses a broken rhythm that is as the very rhythm of life itself, and a cadence that catches you by the throat, as a terrier catches a rat, and wrings from you the last drop of pity and awe. His skill in avoiding 'the inevitable word' is simply miraculous. He is the despair of the translator. Far be it from me to belittle the devoted labours of Mr. and Mrs. Pegaway, whose monumental translation of the Master's complete works is now drawing to its splendid close. Their promised biography of the murdered grandmother is awaited eagerly by all who take—and which of us does not take?—a breathless interest in Kolniyatschiana. But Mr. and Mrs. Pegaway would be the first to admit that their renderings of the prose and verse they love so well are a wretched substitute for the real thing. I wanted to get the job myself, but they nipped in and got it before me. Thank heaven, they cannot deprive me of the power to read Kolniyatsch in the original Gibrisch and to crow over you who can't.

Of the man himself—for on several occasions I had the privilege and the permit to visit him—I have the pleasantest, most sacred memories. His was a wonderfully vivid and intense personality. The head was beautiful, perfectly conic in form. The eyes were like two revolving lamps, set very close together. The smile was haunting. There was a touch of old-world courtesy in the repression of the evident impulse to spring at one's throat. The voice had notes that recalled M. Mounet-Sully's in the later and more important passages of Oedipe Roi. I remember that he always spoke with the greatest contempt of Mr. and Mrs. Pegaway's translations. He likened them to—but enough! His boom is not yet at the full. A few weeks hence I shall be able to command an even higher price than I could now for my 'Talks with Kolniyatsch.'

No. 2. THE PINES

[Early in the year 1914 Mr. Edmund Gosse told me he was asking certain of his friends to write for him a few words apiece in description of Swinburne as they had known or seen him at one time or another; and he was so good as to wish to include in this gathering a few words by myself. Ifound it hard to be brief without seeming irreverent. I failed in the attempt to make of my subject a snapshot that was not a grotesque. So I took refuge in an ampler scope. I wrote a reminiscential essay. From that essay I made an extract, which I gave to Mr. Gosse. From that extract he made a quotation in his enchanting biography. The words quoted by him reappear here in the midst of the whole essay as I wrote it. I dare not hope they are unashamed of their humble surroundings.—M. B.]

In my youth the suburbs were rather looked down on—I never quite knew why. It was held anomalous, and a matter for merriment, that Swinburne lived in one of them. For my part, had I known as a fact that Catullus was still alive, I should have been as ready to imagine him living in Putney as elsewhere. The marvel would have been merely that he lived. And Swinburne's survival struck as surely as could his have struck in me the chord of wonder.

Not, of course, that he had achieved a feat of longevity. He was far from the Psalmist's limit. Nor was he one of those men whom one associates with the era in which they happened to be young. Indeed, if there was one man belonging less than any other to Mid-Victorian days, Swinburne was that man.

But by the calendar it was in those days that he had blazed—blazed forth with so unexampled a suddenness of splendour; and in the light of that conflagration all that he had since done, much and magnificent though this was, paled. The essential Swinburne was still the earliest. He was and would always be the flammiferous boy of the dim past—a legendary creature, sole kin to the phoenix. It had been impossible that he should ever surpass himself in the artistry that was from the outset his; impossible that he should bring forth rhythms lovelier and greater than those early rhythms, or exercise over them a mastery more than—absolute. Also, it had been impossible that the first wild ardour of spirit should abide unsinkingly in him. Youth goes. And there was not in Swinburne that basis on which a man may in his maturity so build as to make good, in some degree, the loss of what is gone. He was not a thinker: his mind rose ever away from reason to rhapsody; neither was he human. He was a king crowned but not throned. He was a singing bird that could build no nest. He was a youth who could not afford to age. Had he died young, literature would have lost many glories; but none so great as the glories he had already given, nor any such as we should fondly imagine ourselves bereft of by his early death. A great part of Keats' fame rests on our assumption of what he would have done. But—even granting that Keats may have had in him more than had Swinburne of stuff for development—I believe that had he lived on we should think of him as author of the poems that in fact we know. Not philosophy, after all, not humanity, just sheer joyous power of song, is the primal thing in poetry. Ideas, and flesh and blood, are but reserves to be brought up when the poet's youth is going. When the bird can no longer sing in flight, let the nest be ready. After the king has dazzled us with his crown, let him have something to sit down on. But the session on throne or in nest is not the divine period. Had Swinburne's genius been of the kind that solidifies, he would yet at the close of the nineteenth century have been for us young men virtually—though not so definitely as in fact he was—the writer of 'Atalanta in Calydon' and of 'Poems and Ballads.'

Tennyson's death in '98 had not taken us at all by surprise. We had been fully aware that he was alive. He had always been careful to keep himself abreast of the times. Anything that came along—the Nebular Hypothesis at one moment, the Imperial Institute at another—won mention from his Muse. He had husbanded for his old age that which he had long ago inherited: middle age. If in our mourning for him there really was any tincture of surprise, this was due to merely the vague sense that he had in the fullness of time died rather prematurely: his middle-age might have been expected to go on flourishing for ever. But assuredly Tennyson dead laid no such strain on our fancy as Swinburne living.

It is true that Swinburne did, from time to time, take public notice of current affairs; but what notice he took did but seem to mark his remoteness from them, from us. The Boers, I remember, were the theme of a sonnet which embarrassed even their angriest enemies in our midst. He likened them, if I remember rightly, to 'hell-hounds foaming at the jaws.' This was by some people taken as a sign that he had fallen away from that high generosity of spirit which had once been his. To me it meant merely that he thought of poor little England writhing under the heel of an alien despotism, just as, in the days when he really was interested in such matters, poor little Italy had writhen. I suspect, too, that the first impulse to write about the Boers came not from the Muse within, but from Theodore Watts-Dunton without.... 'Now, Algernon, we're at war, you know—at war with the Boers. I don't want to bother you at all, but I do think, my dear old friend, you oughtn't to let slip this opportunity of,' etc., etc.

Some such hortation is easily imaginable by any one who saw the two old friends together. The first time I had this honour, this sight for lasting and affectionate memory, must have been in the Spring of '99. In those days Theodore Watts (he had but recently taken on the -Dunton) was still something of a gad-about. I had met him here and there, he had said in his stentorian tones pleasant things to me about my writing, I sent him a new little book of mine, and in acknowledging this he asked me to come down to Putney and 'have luncheon and meet Swinburne.' Meet Catullus!

On the day appointed 'I came as one whose feet half linger.' It is but a few steps from the railway-station in Putney High Street to No. 2. The Pines. I had expected a greater distance to the sanctuary—a walk in which to compose my mind and prepare myself for initiation. I laid my hand irresolutely against the gate of the bleak trim front-garden, I withdrew my hand, I went away. Out here were all the aspects of common modern life. In there was Swinburne. A butcher-boy went by, whistling. He was not going to see Swinburne. He could afford to whistle. I pursued my dilatory course up the slope of Putney, but at length it occurred to me that unpunctuality would after all be an imperfect expression of reverence, and I retraced my footsteps.

No. 2—prosaic inscription! But as that front-door closed behind me I had the instant sense of having slipped away from the harsh light of the ordinary and contemporary into the dimness of an odd, august past. Here, in this dark hall, the past was the present. Here loomed vivid and vital on the walls those women of Rossetti whom I had known but as shades. Familiar to me in small reproductions by photogravure, here they themselves were, life-sized, 'with curled-up lips and amorous hair' done in the original warm crayon, all of them intently looking down on me while I took off my overcoat—all wondering who was this intruder from posterity. That they hung in the hall, evidently no more than an overflow, was an earnest of packed plenitude within. The room I was ushered into was a back-room, a dining-room, looking on to a good garden. It was, in form and 'fixtures,' an inalienably Mid-Victorian room, and held its stolid own in the riot of Rossettis. Its proportions, its window-sash bisecting the view of garden, its folding-doors (through which I heard the voice of Watts-Dunton booming mysteriously in the front room), its mantel-piece, its gas-brackets, all proclaimed that nothing ever would seduce them from their allegiance to Martin Tupper. 'Nor me from mine,' said the sturdy cruet-stand on the long expanse of table-cloth. The voice of Watts-Dunton ceased suddenly, and a few moments later its owner appeared. He had been dictating, he explained. 'A great deal of work on hand just now—a great deal of work.'... I remember that on my subsequent visits he was always, at the moment of my arrival, dictating, and always greeted me with that phrase, 'A great deal of work on hand just now.' I used to wonder what work it was, for he published little enough. But I never ventured to inquire, and indeed rather cherished the mystery: it was a part of the dear little old man; it went with the something gnome-like about his swarthiness and chubbiness—went with the shaggy hair that fell over the collar of his eternally crumpled frock-coat, the shaggy eyebrows that overhung his bright little brown eyes, the shaggy moustache that hid his small round chin. It was a mystery inherent in the richly-laden atmosphere of The Pines....

While I stood talking to Watts-Dunton—talking as loudly as he, for he was very deaf—I enjoyed the thrill of suspense in watching the door through which would appear—Swinburne. I asked after Mr. Swinburne's health. Watts-Dunton said it was very good: 'He always goes out for his long walk in the morning—wonderfully active. Active in mind, too. But I'm afraid you won't be able to get into touch with him. He's almost stone-deaf, poor fellow—almost stone-deaf now.' He changed the subject, and I felt I must be careful not to seem interested in Swinburne exclusively. I spoke of 'Aylwin.' The parlourmaid brought in the hot dishes. The great moment was at hand.

Nor was I disappointed. Swinburne's entry was for me a great moment. Here, suddenly visible in the flesh, was the legendary being and divine singer. Here he was, shutting the door behind him as might anybody else, and advancing—a strange small figure in grey, having an air at once noble and roguish, proud and skittish. My name was roared to him. In shaking his hand, I bowed low, of course—a bow de coeur; and he, in the old aristocratic manner, bowed equally low, but with such swiftness that we narrowly escaped concussion. You do not usually associate a man of genius, when you see one, with any social class; and, Swinburne being of an aspect so unrelated as it was to any species of human kind, I wondered the more that almost the first impression he made on me, or would make on any one, was that of a very great gentleman indeed. Not of an old gentleman, either. Sparse and straggling though the grey hair was that fringed the immense pale dome of his head, and venerably haloed though he was for me by his greatness, there was yet about him something—boyish? girlish? childish, rather; something of a beautifully well-bred child. But he had the eyes of a god, and the smile of an elf. In figure, at first glance, he seemed almost fat; but this was merely because of the way he carried himself, with his long neck strained so tightly back that he all receded from the waist upwards. I noticed afterwards that this deportment made the back of his jacket hang quite far away from his legs; and so small and sloping were his shoulders that the jacket seemed ever so likely to slip right off. I became aware, too, that when he bowed he did not unbend his back, but only his neck—the length of the neck accounting for the depth of the bow. His hands were tiny, even for his size, and they fluttered helplessly, touchingly, unceasingly.

Directly after my introduction, we sat down to the meal. Of course I had never hoped to 'get into touch with him' reciprocally. Quite apart from his deafness, I was too modest to suppose he could be interested in anything I might say. But—for I knew he had once been as high and copious a singer in talk as in verse—I had hoped to hear utterances from him. And it did not seem that my hope was to be fulfilled. Watts-Dunton sat at the head of the table, with a huge and very Tupperesque joint of roast mutton in front of him, Swinburne and myself close up to him on either side. He talked only to me. This was the more tantalising because Swinburne seemed as though he were bubbling over with all sorts of notions. Not that he looked at either of us. He smiled only to himself, and to his plateful of meat, and to the small bottle of Bass's pale ale that stood before him—ultimate allowance of one who had erst clashed cymbals in Naxos. This small bottle he eyed often and with enthusiasm, seeming to waver between the rapture of broaching it now and the grandeur of having it to look forward to. It made me unhappy to see what trouble he had in managing his knife and fork. Watts-Dunton told me on another occasion that this infirmity of the hands had been lifelong—had begun before Eton days. The Swinburne family had been alarmed by it and had consulted a specialist, who said that it resulted from 'an excess of electric vitality,' and that any attempt to stop it would be harmful. So they had let it be. I have known no man of genius who had not to pay, in some affliction or defect either physical or spiritual, for what the gods had given him. Here, in this fluttering of his tiny hands, was a part of the price that Swinburne had to pay. No doubt he had grown accustomed to it many lustres before I met him, and I need not have felt at all unhappy at what I tried not to see. He, evidently, was quite gay, in his silence-and in the world that was for him silent. I had, however, the maddening suspicion that he would have liked to talk. Why wouldn't Watts-Dunton roar him an opportunity? I felt I had been right perhaps in feeling that the lesser man was—no, not jealous of the greater whom he had guarded so long and with such love, but anxious that he himself should be as fully impressive to visitors as his fine gifts warranted. Not, indeed, that he monopolised the talk. He seemed to regard me as a source of information about all the latest 'movements,' and I had to shout banalities while he munched his mutton—banalities whose one saving grace for me was that they were inaudible to Swinburne. Had I met Swinburne's gaze, I should have faltered. Now and again his shining light-grey eyes roved from the table, darting this way and that—across the room, up at the ceiling, out of the window; only never at us. Somehow this aloofness gave no hint of indifference. It seemed to be, rather, a point in good manners—the good manners of a child 'sitting up to table,' not 'staring,' not 'asking questions,' and reflecting great credit on its invaluable old nurse. The child sat happy in the wealth of its inner life; the child was content not to speak until it were spoken to; but, but, I felt it did want to he spoken to. And, at length, it was.

So soon as the mutton had been replaced by the apple-pie, Watts-Dunton leaned forward and 'Well, Algernon,' he roared, 'how was it on the Heath to-day?' Swinburne, who had meekly inclined his ear to the question, now threw back his head, uttering a sound that was like the cooing of a dove, and forthwith, rapidly, ever so musically, he spoke to us of his walk; spoke not in the strain of a man who had been taking his daily exercise on Putney Heath, but rather in that of a Peri who had at long last been suffered to pass through Paradise. And rather than that he spoke would I say that he cooingly and flutingly sang of his experience. The wonders of this morning's wind and sun and clouds were expressed in a flow of words so right and sentences so perfectly balanced that they would have seemed pedantic had they not been clearly as spontaneous as the wordless notes of a bird in song. The frail, sweet voice rose and fell, lingered, quickened, in all manner of trills and roulades. That he himself could not hear it, seemed to me the greatest loss his deafness inflicted on him. One would have expected this disability to mar the music; but it didn't; save that now and again a note would come out metallic and over-shrill, the tones were under good control. The whole manner and method had certainly a strong element of oddness; but no one incapable of condemning as unmanly the song of a lark would have called it affected. I had met young men of whose enunciation Swinburne's now reminded me. In them the thing had always irritated me very much; and I now became sure that it had been derived from people who had derived it in old Balliol days from Swinburne himself. One of the points familiar to me in such enunciation was the habit of stressing extremely, and lackadaisically dwelling on, some particular syllable. In Swinburne this trick was delightful—because it wasn't a trick, but a need of his heart. Well do I remember his ecstasy of emphasis and immensity of pause when he described how he had seen in a perambulator on the Heath to-day 'the most BEAUT—iful babbie ever beheld by mortal eyes.' For babies, as some of his later volumes testify, he had a sort of idolatry. After Mazzini had followed Landor to Elysium, and Victor Hugo had followed Mazzini, babies were what among live creatures most evoked Swinburne's genius for self-abasement. His rapture about this especial 'babbie' was such as to shake within me my hitherto firm conviction that, whereas the young of the brute creation are already beautiful at the age of five minutes, the human young never begin to be so before the age of three years. I suspect Watts-Dunton of having shared my lack of innate enthusiasm. But it was one of Swinburne's charms, as I was to find, that he took for granted every one's delight in what he himself so fervidly delighted in. He could as soon have imagined a man not loving the very sea as not doting on the aspect of babies and not reading at least one play by an Elizabethan or Jacobean dramatist every day.

I forget whether it was at this my first meal or at another that he described a storm in which, one night years ago, with Watts-Dunton, he had crossed the Channel. The rhythm of his great phrases was as the rhythm of those waves, and his head swayed in accordance to it like the wave-rocked boat itself. He hymned in memory the surge and darkness, the thunder and foam and phosphorescence—'You remember, Theodore? You remember the PHOS—phorescence?'—all so beautifully and vividly that I almost felt stormbound and in peril of my life. To disentangle one from another of the several occasions on which I heard him talk is difficult because the procedure was so invariable: Watts-Dunton always dictating when I arrived, Swinburne always appearing at the moment of the meal, always the same simple and substantial fare, Swinburne never allowed to talk before the meal was half over. As to this last point, I soon realised that I had been quite unjust in suspecting Watts-Dunton of selfishness. It was simply a sign of the care with which he watched over his friend's welfare. Had Swinburne been admitted earlier to the talk, he would not have taken his proper quantity of roast mutton. So soon, always, as he had taken that, the embargo was removed, the chance was given him. And, swiftly though he embraced the chance, and much though he made of it in the courses of apple-pie and of cheese, he seemed touchingly ashamed of 'holding forth.' Often, before he had said his really full say on the theme suggested by Watts-Dunton's loud interrogation, he would curb his speech and try to eliminate himself, bowing his head over his plate; and then, when he had promptly been brought in again, he would always try to atone for his inhibiting deafness by much reference and deference to all that we might otherwise have to say. 'I hope,' he would coo to me, 'my friend Watts-Dunton, who'—and here he would turn and make a little bow to Watts-Dunton—'is himself a scholar, will bear me out when I say'—or 'I hardly know,' he would flute to his old friend, 'whether Mr. Beerbohm'—here a bow to me—'will agree with me in my opinion of some delicate point in Greek prosody or some incident in an old French romance I had never heard of.

On one occasion, just before the removal of the mutton, Watts-Dunton had been asking me about an English translation that had been made of M. Rostand's 'Cyrano de Bergerac.' He then took my information as the match to ignite the Swinburnian tinder. 'Well, Algernon, it seems that "Cyrano de Bergerac"—but this first spark was enough: instantly Swinburne was praising the works of Cyrano de Bergerac. Of M. Rostand he may have heard, but him he forgot. Indeed I never heard Swinburne mention a single contemporary writer. His mind ranged and revelled always in the illustrious or obscure past. To him the writings of Cyrano de Bergerac were as fresh as paint—as fresh as to me, alas, was the news of their survival. Of course, of course, you have read "L'Histoire Comique des •tats et des Empires de la Lune"?' I admitted, by gesture and facial expression, that I had not. Whereupon he reeled out curious extracts from that allegory— 'almost as good as "Gulliver"'—with a memorable instance of the way in which the traveller to the moon was shocked by the conversation of the natives, and the natives' sense of propriety was outraged by the conversation of the traveller.

In life, as in (that for him more truly actual thing) literature, it was always the preterit that enthralled him. Of any passing events, of anything the newspapers were full of, never a word from him; and I should have been sorry if there had been. But I did, through the medium of Watts-Dunton, sometimes start him on topics that might have led him to talk of Rossetti and other old comrades. For me the names of those men breathed the magic of the past, just as it was breathed for me by Swinburne's presence. For him, I suppose, they were but a bit of the present, and the mere fact that they had dropped out of it was not enough to hallow them. He never mentioned them. But I was glad to see that he revelled as wistfully in the days just before his own as I in the days just before mine. He recounted to us things he had been told in his boyhood by an aged aunt, or great-aunt—'one of the Ashburnhams'; how, for example, she had been taken by her mother to a county ball, a distance of many miles, and, on the way home through the frosty and snowy night, the family-coach had suddenly stopped: there was a crowd of dark figures in the way...at which point Swinburne stopped too, before saying, with an ineffable smile and in a voice faint with appreciation, 'They were burying a suicide at the crossroads.'

Vivid as this Hogarthian night-scene was to me, I saw beside it another scene: a great panelled room, a grim old woman in a high-backed chair, and, restless on a stool at her feet an extraordinary little nephew with masses of auburn hair and with tiny hands clasped in supplication—'Tell me more, Aunt Ashburnham, tell me more!'

And now, clearlier still, as I write in these after-years, do I see that dining-room of The Pines; the long white stretch of table-cloth, with Swinburne and Watts-Dunton and another at the extreme end of it; Watts-Dunton between us, very low down over his plate, very cosy and hirsute, and rather like the dormouse at that long tea-table which Alice found in Wonderland. I see myself sitting there wide-eyed, as Alice sat. And, had the hare been a great poet, and the hatter a great gentleman, and neither of them mad but each only very odd and vivacious, I might see Swinburne as a glorified blend of those two.

When the meal ended—for, alas! it was not, like that meal in Wonderland, unending—Swinburne would dart round the table, proffer his hand to me, bow deeply, bow to

Watts-Dunton also, and disappear. 'He always walks in the morning, writes in the afternoon, and reads in the evening,' Watts-Dunton would say with a touch of tutorial pride in this regimen.

That parting bow of Swinburne to his old friend was characteristic of his whole relation to him. Cronies though they were, these two, knit together with bonds innumerable, the greater man was always aux petits soins for the lesser, treating him as a newly-arrived young guest might treat an elderly host. Some twenty years had passed since that night when, ailing and broken—thought to be nearly dying, Watts-Dunton told me—Swinburne was brought in a four-wheeler to The Pines. Regular private nursing-homes either did not exist in those days or were less in vogue than they are now. The Pines was to he a sort of private nursing-home for Swinburne. It was a good one. He recovered. He was most grateful to his friend and saviour. He made as though to depart, was persuaded to stay a little longer, and then a little longer than that. But I rather fancy that, to the last, he never did, in the fullness of his modesty and good manners, consent to regard his presence as a matter of course, or as anything but a terminable intrusion and obligation. His bow seemed always to convey that.

Swinburne having gone from the room, in would come the parlourmaid. The table was cleared, the fire was stirred, two leather arm-chairs were pushed up to the hearth. Watts-Dunton wanted gossip of the present. I wanted gossip of the great past. We settled down for a long, comfortable afternoon together.

Only once was the ritual varied. Swinburne (I was told before luncheon) had expressed a wish to show me his library. So after the meal he did not bid us his usual adieu, but with much courtesy invited us and led the way. Up the staircase he then literally bounded—three, literally three, stairs at a time. I began to follow at the same rate, but immediately slackened speed for fear that Watts-Dunton behind us might be embittered at sight of so much youth and legerity. Swinburne waited on the threshold to receive us, as it were, and pass us in. Watts-Dunton went and ensconced himself snugly in a corner. The sun had appeared after a grey morning, and it pleasantly flooded this big living-room whose walls were entirely lined with the mellow backs of books. Here, as host, among his treasures, Swinburne was more than ever attractive. He was as happy as was any mote in the sunshine about him; and the fluttering of his little hands, and feet too, was but as a token of so much felicity. He looked older, it is true, in the strong light. But these added years made only more notable his youngness of heart. An illustrious bibliophile among his books? A birthday child, rather, among his toys.

Proudly he explained to me the general system under which the volumes were ranged in this or that division of shelves. Then he conducted me to a chair near the window, left me there, flew away, flew up the rungs of a mahogany ladder, plucked a small volume, and in a twinkling was at my side: 'This, I think, will please you!' It did. It had a beautifully engraved title-page and a pleasing scent of old, old leather. It was editio princeps of a play by some lesser Elizabethan or Jacobean. 'Of course you know it?' my host fluted.

How I wished I could say that I knew it and loved it well! I revealed to him (for by speaking very loudly towards his inclined head I was able to make him hear) that I had not read it. He envied any one who had such pleasure in store. He darted to the ladder, and came back thrusting gently into my hands another volume of like date: 'Of course you know this?'

Again I had to confess that I did not, and to shout my appreciation of the fount of type, the margins, the binding. He beamed agreement, and fetched another volume. Archly he indicated the title, cooing, 'You are a lover of this, I hope?' And again I was shamed by my inexperience.

I did not pretend to know this particular play, but my tone implied that I had always been meaning to read it and had always by some mischance been prevented. For his sake as well as my own I did want to acquit myself passably. I wanted for him the pleasure of seeing his joys shared by a representative, however humble, of the common world. I turned the leaves caressingly, looking from them to him, while he dilated on the beauty of this and that scene in the play. Anon he fetched another volume, and another, always with the same faith that this was a favourite of mine. I quibbled, I evaded, I was very enthusiastic and uncomfortable. It was with intense relief that I beheld the title-page of yet another volume which (silently, this time) he laid before me—The Country Wench. 'This of course I have read,' I heartily shouted.

Swinburne stepped back. 'You have? You have read it? Where?' he cried, in evident dismay.

Something was wrong. Had I not, I quickly wondered, read this play? 'Oh yes,' I shouted, 'I have read it.'

'But when? Where?' entreated Swinburne, adding that he had supposed it to be the sole copy extant.

I floundered. I wildly said I thought I must have read it years ago in the Bodleian. 'Theodore! Do you hear this? It seems that they have now a copy of "The Country Wench" in the Bodleian! Mr. Beerbohm found one there—oh when? in what year?' he appealed to me.

I said it might have been six, seven, eight years ago. Swinburne knew for certain that no copy had been there twelve years ago, and was surprised that he had not heard of the acquisition. 'They might have told me,' he wailed.

I sacrificed myself on the altar of sympathy. I admitted that I might have been mistaken—must have been—must have confused this play with some other. I dipped into the pages and 'No,' I shouted, 'this I have never read.'

His equanimity was restored. He was up the ladder and down

again, showing me further treasures with all pride and ardour. At length, Watts-Dunton, afraid that his old friend would tire himself, arose from his corner, and presently he and I went downstairs to the dining-room. It was in the course of our session together that there suddenly flashed across my mind the existence of a play called 'The Country Wife,' by—wasn't it Wycherley? I had once read it—or read something about it.... But this matter I kept to myself. I thought I had appeared fool enough already.

I loved those sessions in that Tupperossettine dining-room, lair of solid old comfort and fervid old romanticism. Its odd duality befitted well its owner. The distinguished critic and poet, Rossetti's closest friend and Swinburne's, had been, for a while, in the dark ages, a solicitor; and one felt he had been a good one. His frock-coat, though the Muses had crumpled it, inspired confidence in his judgment of other things than verse. But let there be no mistake. He was no mere bourgeois parnassien, as his enemies insinuated. No doubt he had been very useful to men of genius, in virtue of qualities they lacked, but the secret of his hold on them was in his own rich nature. He was not only a born man of letters, he was a deeply emotional human being whose appeal was as much to the heart as to the head. The romantic Celtic mysticism of 'Aylwin,' with its lack of fashionable Celtic nebulosity, lends itself, if you will, to laughter, though personally I saw nothing funny in it: it seemed to me, before I was in touch with the author, a work of genuine expression from within; and that it truly was so I presently knew. The mysticism of Watts-Dunton (who, once comfortably settled at the fireside, knew no reserve) was in contrast with the frock-coat and the practical abilities; but it was essential, and they were of the surface. For humorous Rossetti, I daresay, the very contrast made Theodore's company the more precious. He himself had assuredly been, and the memory of him still was, the master-fact in Watts-Dunton's life. 'Algernon' was as an adopted child, 'Gabriel' as a long-lost only brother. As he was to the outer world of his own day, so too to posterity Rossetti, the man, is conjectural and mysterious. We know that he was in his prime the most inspiring and splendid of companions. But we know this only by faith. The evidence is as vague as it is emphatic. Of the style and substance of not a few great talkers in the past we can piece together some more or less vivid and probably erroneous notion. But about Rossetti nothing has been recorded in such a way as to make him even faintly emerge. I suppose he had in him what reviewers seem to find so often in books a quality that defies analysis. Listening to Watts-Dunton, I was always in hope that when next the long-lost turned up—for he was continually doing so—in the talk, I should see him, hear him, and share the rapture. But the revelation was not to be. You might think that to hear him called 'Gabriel' would have given me a sense of propinquity. But I felt no nearer to him than you feel to the Archangel who bears that name and no surname.

It was always when Watts-Dunton spoke carelessly, casually, of some to me illustrious figure in the past, that I had the sense of being wafted right into that past and plumped down in the very midst of it. When he spoke with reverence of this and that great man whom he had known, he did not thus waft and plump me; for I, too, revered those names. But I had the magical transition whenever one of the immortals was mentioned in the tone of those who knew him before he had put on immortality. Browning, for example, was a name deeply honoured by me. 'Browning, yes,' said Watts-Dunton, in the course of an afternoon, 'Browning,' and he took a sip of the steaming whisky-toddy that was a point in our day's ritual. 'I was a great diner-out in the old times. I used to dine out every night in the week. Browning was a great diner-out, too. We were always meeting. What a pity he went on writing all those plays! He hadn't any gift for drama—none. I never could understand why he took to play-writing.' He wagged his head, gazing regretfully into the fire, and added, 'Such a clever fellow, too!'

Whistler, though alive and about, was already looked to as a hierarch by the young. Not so had he been looked to by Rossetti. The thrill of the past was always strong in me when Watts-Dunton mentioned—seldom without a guffaw did he mention—'Jimmy Whistler.' I think he put in the surname because 'that fellow' had not behaved well to Swinburne. But he could not omit the nickname, because it was impossible for him to feel the right measure of resentment against 'such a funny fellow.' As heart-full of old hates as of old loves was Watts-Dunton, and I take it as high testimony to the charm of Whistler's quaintness that Watts-Dunton did not hate him. You may be aware that Swinburne, in '88, wrote for one of the monthly reviews a criticism of the 'Ten O'Clock' lecture. He paid courtly compliments to Whistler as a painter, but joined issue with his theories. Straightway there appeared in the World a little letter from Whistler, deriding 'one Algernon Swinburne—outsider—Putney.' It was not in itself a very pretty or amusing letter; and still less so did it seem in the light of the facts which Watts-Dunton told me in some such words as these: After he'd published that lecture of his, Jimmy Whistler had me to dine with him at Kettner's or somewhere. He said "Now, Theodore, I want you to do me a favour." He wanted to get me to get Swinburne to write an article about his lecture. I said "No, Jimmy Whistler, I can't ask Algernon to do that. He's got a great deal of work on hand just now—a great deal of work. And besides, this sort of thing wouldn't be at all in his line.' But Jimmy Whistler went on appealing to me. He said it would do him no end of good if Swinburne wrote about him. And—well, I half gave in: I said perhaps I would mention the matter to Algernon. And next day I did. I could see Algernon didn't want to do it at all. But—well, there, he said he'd do it to please me. And he did it. And then Jimmy Whistler published that letter. A very shabby trick—very shabby indeed.' Of course I do not vouch for the exact words in which Watts-Dunton told me this tale; but this was exactly the tale he told me. I expressed my astonishment. He added that of course he 'never wanted to see the fellow again after that, and never did.' But presently, after a long gaze into the coals, he emitted a chuckle, as for earlier memories of 'such a funny fellow.' One quite recent memory he had, too. 'When I took on the name of Dunton, I had a note from him. Just this, with his butterfly signature: Theodore! What's Dunton? That was very good—very good.... But, of course,' he added gravely,

'I took no notice.' And no doubt, quite apart from the difficulty of finding an answer in the same vein, he did well in not replying. Loyalty to Swinburne forbade. But I see a certain pathos in the unanswered message. It was a message from the hand of an old jester, but also, I think, from the heart of an old man—a signal waved jauntily, but in truth wistfully, across the gulf of years and estrangement; and one could wish it had not been ignored.

Some time after Whistler died I wrote for one of the magazines an appreciation of his curious skill in the art of writing. Watts-Dunton told me he had heard of this from Swinburne. 'I myself,' he said, 'very seldom read the magazines. But Algernon always has a look at them.' There was something to me very droll, and cheery too, in this picture of the illustrious recluse snatching at the current issues of our twaddle. And I was immensely pleased at hearing that my article had 'interested him very much.' I inwardly promised myself that as soon as I reached home I would read the article, to see just how it might have struck Swinburne. When in due course I did this, I regretted the tone of the opening sentences, in which I declared myself 'no book-lover' and avowed a preference for 'an uninterrupted view of my fellow-creatures.' I felt that had I known my article would meet the eye of Swinburne I should have cut out that overture. I dimly remembered a fine passage in one of his books of criticism—something (I preferred not to verify it) about 'the dotage of duncedom which cannot perceive, or the impudence of insignificance so presumptuous as to doubt, that the elements of life and literature are indivisibly mingled one in another, and that he to whom books are less real than life will assuredly find in men and women as little reality as in his accursed crassness he deserves to discover.' I quailed, I quailed. But mine is a resilient nature, and I promptly reminded myself that Swinburne's was a very impersonal one: he would not think the less highly of me, for he never had thought about me in any way whatsoever. All was well. I knew I could revisit The Pines, when next Watts-Dunton should invite me, without misgiving. And to this day I am rather proud of having been mentioned, though not by name, and not consciously, and unfavourably, by Swinburne.

I wonder that I cannot recall more than I do recall of those hours at The Pines. It is odd how little remains to a man of his own past—how few minutes of even his memorable hours are not clean forgotten, and how few seconds in any one of those minutes can be recaptured... I am middle-aged, and have lived a vast number of seconds. Subtract one third of these, for one mustn't count sleep as life. The residual number is still enormous. Not a single one of those seconds was unimportant to me in its passage. Many of them bored me, of course; but even boredom is a positive state: one chafes at it and hates it; strange that one should afterwards forget it! And stranger still that of one's actual happinesses and unhappinesses so tiny and tattered a remnant clings about one! Of those hours at The Pines, of that past within a past, there was not a minute nor a second that I did not spend with pleasure. Memory is a great artist, we are told; she selects and rejects and shapes and so on. No doubt. Elderly persons would be utterly intolerable if they remembered everything. Everything, nevertheless, is just what they themselves would like to remember, and just what they would like to tell to everybody. Be sure that the Ancient Mariner, though he remembered quite as much as his audience wanted to hear, and rather more, about the albatross and the ghastly crew, was inwardly raging at the sketchiness of his own mind; and believe me that his stopping only one of three was the merest oversight. I should like to impose on the world many tomes about The Pines.

But, scant though my memories are of the moments there, very full and warm in me is the whole fused memory of the two dear old men that lived there. I wish I had Watts-Dunton's sure faith in meetings beyond the grave. I am glad I do not disbelieve that people may so meet. I like to think that some day in Elysium I shall—not without diffidence—approach those two and reintroduce myself. I can see just how courteously Swinburne will bow over my hand, not at all remembering who I am. Watts-Dunton will remember me after a moment: 'Oh, to be sure, yes indeed! I've a great deal of work on hand just now—a great deal of work, but' we shall sit down together on the asphodel, and I cannot but think we shall have whisky-toddy even there. He will not have changed. He will still be shaggy and old and chubby, and will wear the same frock-coat, with the same creases in it. Swinburne, on the other hand, will be quite, quite young, with a full mane of flaming auburn locks, and no clothes to hinder him from plunging back at any moment into the shining Elysian waters from which he will have just emerged. I see him skim lightly away into that element. On the strand is sitting a man of noble and furrowed brow. It is Mazzini, still thinking of Liberty. And anon the tiny young English amphibian comes ashore to fling himself dripping at the feet of the patriot and to carol the Republican ode he has composed in the course of his swim. 'He's wonderfully active—active in mind and body,' Watts-Dunton says to me. 'I come to the shore now and then, just to see how he's getting on. But I spend most of my time inland. I find I've so much to talk over with Gabriel. Not that he's quite the fellow he was. He always had rather a cult for Dante, you know, and now he's more than ever under the Florentine influence. He lives in a sort of monastery that Dante has here; and there he sits painting imaginary portraits of Beatrice, and giving them all to Dante. But he still has his great moments, and there's no one quite like him—no one. Algernon won't ever come and see him, because that fellow Mazzini's as Anti-Clerical as ever and makes a principle of having nothing to do with Dante. Look!—there's Algernon going into the water again! He'll tire himself out, he'll catch cold, he'll—' and here the old man rises and hurries down to the sea's edge. 'Now, Algernon,' he roars, 'I don't want to interfere with you, but I do think, my dear old friend,'—and then, with a guffaw, he breaks off, remembering that his friend is not deaf now nor old, and that here in Elysium, where no ills are, good advice is not needed.

A LETTER THAT WAS NOT WRITTEN

1914

One morning lately I saw in my newspaper an announcement that enraged me. It was made in the driest, most casual way, as though nobody would care a rap; and this did but whet the wrath I had in knowing that Adam Street, Adelphi, was to be undone. The Tivoli Music Hall, about to be demolished and built anew, was to have a frontage of thirty feet, if you please, in Adam Street. Why? Because the London County Council, with its fixed idea that the happiness of mankind depends on the widening of the Strand, had decreed that the Tivoli's new frontage thereon should be thirty feet further back, and had granted as consolation to the Tivoli the right to spread itself around the corner and wreck the work of the Brothers Adam. Could not this outrage be averted? There sprang from my lips that fiery formula which has sprung from the lips of so many choleric old gentlemen in the course of the past hundred years and more: 'I shall write to The Times.'

If Adam Street were a thing apart I should have been stricken enough, heaven knows, at thought of its beauty going, its dear tradition being lost. But not as an unrelated masterpiece was Adam Street built by the Brothers whose name it bears. An integral part it is in their noble design of the Adelphi. It is the very key to the Adelphi, the well-ordained initiation for us into that small, matchless quarter of London, where peace and dignity do still reign—peace the more beatific, and dignity the finer, by instant contrast with the chaos of hideous sounds and sights hard by. What man so gross that, passing out of the Strand into Adam Street, down the mild slope to the river, he has not cursed the age he was born into—or blessed it because the Adelphi cannot in earlier days have had for any one this fullness of peculiar magic? Adam Street is not so beautiful as the serene Terrace it goes down to, nor so curiously grand as crook-backed John Street. But the Brothers did not mean it to be so. They meant it just as an harmonious 'lead' to those inner glories of their scheme. Ruin that approach, and how much else do you ruin of a thing which—done perfectly by masters, and done by them here as nowhere else could they have done it—ought to be guarded by us very jealously! How to raise on this irregular and 'barbarous' ground a quarter that should be 'polite', congruous in tone with the smooth river beyond it—this was the irresistible problem the Brothers set themselves and slowly, coolly, perfectly solved. So long as the Adelphi remains to us, a microcosm of the eighteenth century is ours. If there is any meaning in the word sacrilege—

That, I remember, was the beginning of one of the sentences I composed while I paced my room, thinking out my letter to The Times. I rejected that sentence. I rejected scores of others. They were all too vehement. Though my facility for indignation is not (I hope) less than that of my fellows, I never had written to The Times. And now, though I flattered myself I knew how the thing ought to be done, I was unsure that I could do it. Was I beginning too late? Restraint was the prime effect to be aimed at. If you are intemperate, you don't convince. I wanted to convince the readers of The Times that the violation of the Adelphi was a thing to be prevented at all costs. Soberness of statement, a simple, direct, civic style, with only an underthrob of personal emotion, were what I must at all costs achieve. Not too much of mere aesthetics, either, nor of mere sentiment for the past. No more than a brief eulogy of 'those admirably proportioned streets so familiar to all students of eighteenth century architecture,' and perhaps a passing reference to 'the shades of Dr. Johnson, Garrick, Hannah More, Sir Joshua Reynolds. Topham Beauclerk, and how many others!' The sooner my protest were put in terms of commerce, the better for my cause. The more clearly I were to point out that such antiquities as the Adelphi are as a magnet to the moneyed tourists of America and Europe, the likelier would my readers be to shudder at 'a proposal which, if carried into effect, will bring discredit on all concerned and will in some measure justify Napoleon's hitherto-unjustified taunt that we are a nation of shopkeepers.—I am, Sir, your obedient servant'—good! I sat down to a table and wrote out that conclusion, and then I worked backwards, keeping well in view the idea of 'restraint.' But that quality which is little sister to restraint, and is yet far more repulsive to the public mind than vehemence, emerged to misguide my pen. Irony, in fact, played the deuce. I found myself writing that a nation which, in its ardour for beauty and its reverence for great historic associations, has lately disbursed after only a few months' hesitation œ250,000 to save the Crystal Palace, where the bank holidays of millions of toilers have been spoilt by the utter gloom and nullity of the place—a nullity and gloom that will, however and of course, be dispelled so soon as the place is devoted to permanent exhibitions of New Zealand pippins, Rhodesian tobacco, Australian mutton, Canadian snow-shoes, and other glories of Empire—might surely not be asked in vain to'—but I deleted that sentence, and tried another in another vein. My desire to be straightforward did but topple me into excess of statement. My sorrow for the Adelphi came out as sentimentality, my anger against the authorities as vulgar abuse. Only the urgency of my cause upheld me. I would get my letter done somehow and post it. But there flitted through my mind that horrid doubt which has flitted through the minds of so many choleric old gentlemen in the course of the past hundred years and more: 'Will The Times put my letter in?'

If The Times wouldn't, what then? At least my conscience would be clear: I should have done what I could to save my beloved quarter. But the process of doing it was hard and tedious, and I was glad of the little respite presented by the thought that I must, before stating my case thoroughly, revisit Adam Street itself, to gauge precisely the extent of the mischief threatened there. On my way to the Strand I met an old friend, one of my links with whom is his love of the Adams' work. He had not read the news, and I am sorry to say that I, in my selfish agitation, did not break it to him gently. Rallying, he accompanied me on my sombre quest.

I had forgotten there was a hosier's shop next to the Tivoli, at the corner of the right-hand side of Adam Street. We turned past it, and were both of us rather surprised that there were other shops down that side. They ought never to have been allowed there; but there they were; and of course, I felt, it was the old façades above them that really counted. We gazed meanwhile at the façades on the left-hand side, feasting our eyes on the proportions of the pilasters, the windows; the old seemly elegance of it all; the greatness of the manner with the sweet smallness of the scale it wrought on.

'Well,' I said, turning abruptly away, 'to business! Thirty feet—how much, about, is that? My friend moved to the exact corner of the Strand, and then, steadily, methodically, with his eyes to the pavement, walked thirty toe-to-heal paces down Adam Street.

'This,' he said, 'is where the corner of the Tivoli would come'—not 'will come,' observe; I thanked him for that. He passed on, measuring out the thirty additional feet. There was in his demeanour something so finely official that I felt I should at least have the Government on my side.

Thus it was with no sense of taking a farewell look, but rather to survey a thing half-saved already, that I crossed over to the other side of the road, and then, lifting my eyes, and looking to and fro, beheld—what?

I blankly indicated the thing to my friend. How long had it been there, that horrible, long, high frontage of grey stone? It must surely have been there before either of us was born. It seemed to be a very perfect specimen of 1860—1870 architecture—perfect in its pretentious and hateful smugness.

And neither of us had ever known it was there.

Neither of us, therefore, could afford to laugh at the other; nor did either of us laugh at himself; we just went blankly away, and parted. I daresay my friend found presently, as I did, balm in the knowledge that the Tivoli's frontage wouldn't, because it couldn't, be so bad as that which we had just, for the first time, seen.

For me there was another, a yet stronger, balm. And I went as though I trod on air, my heart singing within me. For I had not, after all, to resume my task of writing that letter to The Times.

BOOKS WITHIN BOOKS

1914

They must, I suppose, be classed among biblia abiblia [Greek]. Ignored in the catalogue of any library, not one of them lurking in any uttermost cavern under the reading-room of the British Museum, none of them ever printed even for private circulation, these books written by this and that character in fiction are books only by courtesy and good will.

But how few, after all, the books that are books! Charles Lamb let his kind heart master him when he made that too brief list of books that aren't. Book is an honourable title, not to be conferred lightly. A volume is not necessarily, as Lamb would have had us think, a book because it can be read without difficulty. The test is, whether it was worth reading. Had the author something to set forth? And had he the specific gift for setting it forth in written words? And did he use this rather rare gift conscientiously and to the full? And were his words well and appropriately printed and bound? If you can say Yes to these questions, then only, I submit, is the title of 'book' deserved. If Lamb were alive now, he certainly would draw the line closer than he did. Published volumes were few in his day (though not, of course, few enough). Even he, in all the plenitude of his indulgence, would now have to demur that at least 90 per cent. of the volumes that the publishers thrust on us, so hectically, every spring and autumn, are abiblia [Greek].

What would he have to say of the novels, for example? These

commodities are all very well in their way, no doubt. But let us have no illusions as to what their way is. The poulterer who sells strings of sausages does not pretend that every individual sausage is in itself remarkable. He does not assure us that 'this is a sausage that gives furiously to think,' or 'this is a singularly beautiful and human sausage,' or 'this is undoubtedly the sausage of the year.' Why are such distinctions drawn by the publisher? When he publishes, as he sometimes does, a novel that is a book (or at any rate would be a book if it were decently printed and bound) then by all means let him proclaim its difference—even at the risk of scaring away the majority of readers.

I admit that I myself might be found in that majority. I am shy of masterpieces; nor is this merely because of the many times I have been disappointed at not finding anything at all like what the publishers expected me to find. As a matter of fact, those disappointments are dim in my memory: it is long since I ceased to take publishers' opinions as my guide. I trust now, for what I ought to read, to the advice of a few highly literary friends. But so soon as I am told that I 'must' read this or that, and have replied that I instantly will, I become strangely loth to do anything of the sort. And what I like about books within books is that they never can prick my conscience. It is extraordinarily comfortable that they don't exist.

And yet—for, even as Must implants distaste, so does Can't stir sweet longings—how eagerly would I devour these books within books! What fun, what a queer emotion, to fish out from a fourpenny-box, in a windy by-street, WALTER LORRAINE, by ARTHUR PENDENNIS, or PASSION FLOWERS, by ROSA BUNION! I suppose poor Rosa's muse, so fair and so fervid in Rosa's day, would seem a trifle fatigued now; but what allowances one would make! Lord Steyne said of WALTER LORRAINE that it was 'very clever and wicked.' I fancy we should apply neither epithet now. Indeed, I have always suspected that Pen's maiden effort may have been on a plane with 'The Great Hoggarty Diamond.' Yet I vow would I not skip a line of it.

WHO PUT BACK THE CLOCK? is another work which I especially covet. Poor Gideon Forsyth! He was abominably treated, as Stevenson relates, in the matter of that grand but grisly piano; and I have always hoped that perhaps, in the end, as a sort of recompense, Fate ordained that the novel he had anonymously written should be rescued from oblivion and found by discerning critics to be not at all bad.

"He had never acknowledged it, or only to some intimate friends while it was still in proof; after its appearance and alarming failure, the modesty of the author had become more pressing, and the secret was now likely to be better kept than that of the authorship of 'Waverley.'"

Such an humiliation as Gideon's is the more poignant to me because it is so rare in English fiction. In nine cases out of ten, a book within a book is an immediate, an immense success.

On the whole, our novelists have always tended to optimism—especially they who have written mainly to please their public. It pleases the public to read about any sort of success. The greater, the more sudden and violent the success, the more valuable is it as ingredient in a novel. And since the average novelist lives always in a dream that one of his works will somehow 'catch on' as no other work ever has caught on yet, it is very natural that he should fondly try meanwhile to get this dream realised for him, vicariously, by this or that creature of his fancy. True, he is usually too self-conscious to let this creature achieve his sudden fame and endless fortune through a novel. Usually it is a play that does the trick. In the Victorian time it was almost always a book of poems. Oh for the spacious days of Tennyson and Swinburne! In how many a three-volume novel is mentioned some 'slim octavo' which seems, from the account given, to have been as arresting as 'Poems and Ballads' without being less acceptable than 'Idylls of the King'! These verses were always the anonymous work of some very young, very poor man, who supposed they had fallen still-born from the press until, one day, a week or so after publication, as he walked 'moodily' and 'in a brown study' along the Strand, having given up all hope now that he would ever be in a position to ask Hilda to be his wife, a friend accosted him—'Seen "The Thunderer" this morning? By George, there's a column review of a new book of poems,' etc. In some three-volume novel that I once read at a seaside place, having borrowed it from the little circulating library, there was a young poet whose sudden leap into the front rank has always laid a special hold on my imagination. The name of the novel itself I cannot recall; but I remember the name of the young poet—Aylmer Deane; and the forever unforgettable title of his book of verse was POMENTS: BEING POEMS OF THE MOOD AND THE MOMENT. What would I not give to possess a copy of that work?

Though he had suffered, and though suffering is a sovereign preparation for great work, I did not at the outset foresee that Aylmer Deane was destined to wear the laurel. In real life I have rather a flair for future eminence. In novels I am apt to be wise only after the event. There the young men who do in due course take the town by storm have seldom shown (to my dull eyes) promise. Their spoken thoughts have seemed to me no more profound or pungent than my own. All that is best in these authors goes into their work. But, though I complain of them on this count, I admit that the thrill for me of their triumphs is the more rapturous because every time it catches me unawares. One of the greatest emotions I ever had was from the triumph of THE GIFT OF GIFTS. Of this novel within a novel the author was not a young man at all, but an elderly clergyman whose life had been spent in a little rural parish. He was a dear, simple old man, a widower. He had a large family, a small stipend. Judge, then, of his horror when he found that his eldest son, 'a scholar at Christminster College, Oxbridge,' had run into debt for many hundreds of pounds. Where to turn? The father was too proud to borrow of the neighbourly nobleman who in Oxbridge days had been his 'chum.' Nor had the father ever practised the art of writing. (We are told that 'his sermons were always extempore.') But, years ago, 'he had once thought of writing a novel based on an experience which happened to a friend of his.' This novel, in the fullness of time, he now proceeded to write, though 'without much hope of success.' He knew that he was suffering from heart-disease. But he worked 'feverishly, night after night,' we are told, 'in his old faded dressing-gown, till the dawn mingled with the light of his candle and warned him to snatch a few hours' rest, failing which he would be little able to perform the round of parish duties that awaited him in the daytime.' No wonder he had 'not much hope.' No wonder I had no spark of hope for him. But what are obstacles for but to be overleapt? What avails heart-disease, what avail eld and feverish haste and total lack of literary training, as against the romantic instinct of the lady who created the Rev. Charles Hailing? 'THE GIFT OF GIFTS was acclaimed as a masterpiece by all the first-class critics.' Also, it very soon 'brought in' ten times as much money as was needed to pay off the debts of its author's eldest son. Nor, though Charles Hailing died some months later, are we told that he died from the strain of composition. We are left merely to rejoice at knowing he knew at the last 'that his whole family was provided for.'

I wonder why it is that, whilst these Charles Hailings and Aylmer Deanes delightfully abound in the lower reaches of English fiction, we have so seldom found in the work of our great novelists anything at all about the writing of a great book. It is true, of course, that our great novelists have never had for the idea of literature itself that passion which has always burned in the great French ones. Their own art has never seemed to them the most important and interesting thing in life. Also it is true that they have had other occupations—fox-hunting, preaching, editing magazines, what not. Yet to them literature must, as their own main task, have had a peculiar interest and importance. No fine work can be done without concentration and self-sacrifice and toil and doubt. It is nonsense to imagine that our great novelists have just forged ahead or ambled along, reaching their goal, in the good old English fashion, by sheer divination of the way to it. A fine book, with all that goes to the making of it, is as fine a theme as a novelist can have. But it is a part of English hypocrisy—or, let it be more politely said, English reserve—that, whilst we are fluent enough in grumbling about small inconveniences, we insist on making light of any great difficulties or griefs that may beset us. And just there, I suppose, is the reason why our great novelists have shunned great books as subject-matter. It is fortunate for us (jarring though it is to our patriotic sense) that Mr. Henry James was not born an Englishman, that he was born of a race of specialists—men who are impenitent specialists in whatever they take up, be it sport, commerce, politics, anything. And it is fortunate for us that in Paris, and in the straitest literary sect there, his method began to form itself, and the art of prose fiction became to him a religion. In that art he finds as much inspiration as Swinburne found in the art of poetry. Just as Swinburne was the most learned of our poets, so is Mr. James the most learned of our—let us say 'our'—prose-writers. I doubt whether the heaped total of his admirations would be found to outweigh the least one of the admirations that Swinburne had. But, though he has been a level-headed reader of the works that are good enough for him to praise, his abstract passion for the art of fiction itself has always been fierce and constant. Partly to the Parisian, partly to the American element in him we owe the stories that he, and of 'our' great writers he only, has written about books and the writers of books.

Here, indeed, in these incomparable stories, are imaginary great books that are as real to us as real ones are. Sometimes, as in 'The Author of "Beltraffio,"' a great book itself is the very hero of the story. (We are not told what exactly was the title of that second book which Ambient's wife so hated that she let her child die rather than that he should grow up under the influence of its author; but I have a queer conviction that it was THE DAISIES.) Usually, in these stories, it is through the medium of some ardent young disciple, speaking in the first person, that we become familiar with the great writer. It is thus that we know Hugh Vereker, throughout whose twenty volumes was woven that message, or meaning, that 'figure in the carpet,' which eluded even the elect. It is thus that we know Neil Paraday, the MS. of whose last book was mislaid and lost so tragically, so comically. And it is also through Paraday's disciple that we make incidental acquaintance with Guy Walsingham, the young lady who wrote OBSESSIONS, and with Dora Forbes, the burly man with a red moustache, who wrote THE OTHER WAY ROUND. These two books are the only inferior books mentioned by Mr. James. But stay, I was forgetting THE TOP OF THE TREE, by Amy Evans; and also those nearly forty volumes by Henry St. George. For all the greatness of his success in life, Henry St. George is the saddest of the authors portrayed by Mr. James. His SHADOWMERE was splendid, and its splendour is the measure of his shame—the shame he bore so bravely—in the ruck of his 'output.' He is the only one of those authors who did not do his best. Of him alone it may not be said that he was 'generous and delicate and pursued the prize.' He is a more pathetic figure than even Dencombe, the author of THE MIDDLE YEARS. Dencombe's grievance was against fate, not against himself.

"It had taken too much of his life to produce too little of his art The art had come, but it had come after everything else. 'Ah, for another go!—ah, for a better chance.'... 'A second chance—that's the delusion. There never was to be but one. We work in the dark—we do what we can—we give what we have. Our doubt is our passion and our passion is our task. The rest is the madness of art.'"

The scene of Dencombe's death is one of the most deeply-beautiful things ever done by Mr. James. It is so beautiful as to be hardly sad; it rises and glows and gladdens. It is more exquisite than anything in THE MIDDLE YEARS. No, I will not say that. Mr. James's art can always carry to us the conviction that his characters' books are as fine as his own.

I crave—it may be a foolish whim, but I do crave—ocular evidence for my belief that those books were written and were published. I want to see them all ranged along goodly shelves. A few days ago I sat in one of those libraries which seem to be doorless. Nowhere, to the eye, was broken the array of serried volumes. Each door was flush with the surrounding shelves; across each the edges of the shelves were mimicked; and in the spaces between these edges the backs of books were pasted congruously with the whole effect. Some of these backs had been taken from actual books, others had been made specially and were stamped with facetious titles that rather depressed me. 'Here,' thought I, 'are the shelves on which Dencombe's works ought to be made manifest. And Neil Paraday's too, and Vereker's.' Not Henry St. George's, of course: he would not himself have wished it, poor fellow! I would have nothing of his except SHADOWMERE. But Ray Limbert!—I would have all of his, including a first edition of THE MAJOR KEY, 'that fiery-hearted rose as to which we watched in private the formation of petal after petal, and flame after flame'; and also THE HIDDEN HEART, 'the shortest of his novels, but perhaps the loveliest,' as Mr. James and I have always thought.... How my fingers would hover along these shelves, always just going to alight, but never, lest the spell were broken, alighting!

How well they would look there, those treasures of mine! And, most of them having been issued in the seemly old three-volume form, how many shelves they would fill! But I should find a place certainly for a certain small brown book adorned with a gilt griffin between wheatsheaves. THE PILGRIM'S SCRIP, that delightful though anonymous work of my old friend Austin Absworthy Bearne Feverel. And I should like to find a place for POEMS, by AURORA LEIGH. Mr. Snodgrass's book of verses might grace one of the lower shelves. (What is the title of it? AMELIA'S BOWER, I hazard.) RECOLLECTIONS OF THE LATE LORD BYRON AND OTHERS, by CAPTAIN SUMPH, would be somewhere; for Sumph did, you will be glad to hear, take Shandon's advice and compile a volume. Bungay published it. Indeed, of the books for which I should find room there are a good few that bear the imprimatur of Bungay. DESPERATIN, OR THE FUGITIVE DUCHESS, by THE HON. PERCY Popjoy, was Bungay's; and so, of course, were PASSION

FLOWERS and WALTER LORRAINE. Of the books issued by the rival firm of Bacon I possess but one: MEMOIRS OF THE POISONERS, by DR. SLOCUM. Near to Popjoy's romance would be THE LADY FLABELLA, of which Mrs. Wititterly said to Kate Nickleby, 'So voluptuous is it not—so soft?' WHO PUT BACK THE CLOCK? would have a place of honour (unearned by its own merits?). Among other novels that I could not spare, THE GIFT OF GIFTS would conspicuously gleam. As for POMENTS—ah, I should not be content with one copy of that. Even at the risk of crowding out a host of treasures, I vow I would have a copy of every one of the editions that POMENTS ran through.

THE GOLDEN DRUGGET

1918

Primitive and essential things have great power to touch the heart of the beholder. I mean such things as a man ploughing a field, or sowing or reaping; a girl filling a pitcher from a spring; a young mother with her child; a fisherman mending his nets; a light from a lonely hut on a dark night.

Things such as these are the best themes for poets and painters, and appeal to aught that there may be of painter or poet in any one of us. Strictly, they are not so old as the hills, but they are more significant and eloquent than hills. Hills will outlast them; but hills glacially surviving the life of man on this planet are of as little account as hills tremulous and hot in ages before the life of man had its beginning. Nature is interesting only because of us. And the best symbols of us are such sights as I have just mentioned—sights unalterable by fashion of time or place, sights that in all countries always were and never will not be.

It is true that in many districts nowadays there are elaborate new kinds of machinery for ploughing the fields and reaping the corn. In the most progressive districts of all, I daresay, the very sowing of the grain is done by means of some engine, with better results than could be got by hand. For aught I know, there is a patented invention for catching fish by electricity. It is natural that we should, in some degree, pride ourselves on such triumphs. It is well that we should have poems about them, and pictures of them. But such poems and pictures cannot touch our hearts very deeply. They cannot stir in us the sense of our kinship with the whole dim past and the whole dim future. The ancient Egyptians were great at scientific dodges—very great indeed, nearly as great as we, the archaeologists tell us. Sand buried the memory of those dodges for a rather long time. How are we to know that the glories of our present civilisation will never be lost? The world's coal-mines and oil-fields are exhaustible; and it is not, I am told, by any means certain that scientists will discover any good substitutes for the materials which are necessary to mankind's present pitch of glory. Mankind may, I infer, have to sink back into slow and simple ways, continent be once more separated from continent, nation from nation, village from village. And, even supposing that the present rate of traction and communication and all the rest of it can forever be maintained, is our modern way of life so great a success that mankind will surely never be willing to let it lapse? Doubtless, that present rate can be not only maintained, but also accelerated immensely, in the near future. Will these greater glories be voted, even by the biggest fools, an improvement? We smile already at the people of the early nineteenth century who thought that the vistas opened by applied science were very heavenly. We have travelled far along those vistas. Light is not abundant in them, is it? We are proud of having gone such a long way, but...peradventure, those who come after us will turn back, sooner or later, of their own accord. This is a humbling thought. If the wonders of our civilisation are doomed, we should prefer them to cease through lack of the minerals and mineral products that keep them going. Possibly they are not doomed at all. But this chance counts for little as against the certainty that, whatever happens, the primitive and essential things will never, anywhere, wholly cease, while mankind lasts. And thus it is that Brown's Ode to the Steam Plough, Jones' Sonnet Sequence on the Automatic Reaping Machine, and Robinson's Epic of the Piscicidal Dynamo, leave unstirred the deeper depths of emotion in us. The subjects chosen by these three great poets do not much impress us when we regard them sub specie aeternitatis. Smith has painted nothing more masterly than his picture of a girl turning a hot-water tap. But has he never seen a girl fill a pitcher from a spring? Smithers' picture of a young mother seconding a resolution at a meeting of a Board of Guardians is magnificent, as brushwork. But why not have cut out the Board and put in the baby? I yield to no one in admiration of Smithkins' 'Façade of the Waldorf Hotel by Night, in Peace Time.' But a single light from a lonely hut would have been a finer theme.

I should like to show Smithkins the thing that I call The Golden Drugget. Or rather, as this thing is greatly romantic to me, and that painter is so unfortunate in his surname, I should like Smithkins to find it for himself.

These words are written in war time and in England. There are, I hear, 'lighting restrictions' even on the far Riviera di Levante. I take it that the Golden Drugget is not outspread now-anights across the high dark coast-road between Rapallo and Zoagli. But the lonely wayside inn is still there, doubtless; and its narrow door will again stand open, giving out for wayfarers its old span of brightness into darkness, when peace comes.

It is nothing by daylight, that inn. If anything, it is rather an offence. Steep behind it rise mountains that are grey all over with olive trees, and beneath it, on the other side of the road, the cliff falls sheer to the sea. The road is white, the sea and sky are usually of a deep bright blue, there are many single cypresses among the olives. It is a scene of good colour and noble form. It is a gay and a grand scene, in which the inn, though unassuming, is unpleasing, if you pay attention to it. An ugly little box-like inn. A stuffy-looking and uninviting inn. Salt and tobacco, it announces in faint letters above the door, may be bought there. But one would prefer to buy these things elsewhere. There is a bench outside, and a rickety table with a zinc top to it, and sometimes a peasant or two drinking a glass or two of wine. The proprietress is very unkempt. To Don Quixote she would have seemed a princess, and the inn a castle, and the peasants notable magicians. Don Quixote would have paused here and done something. Not so do I.

By daylight, on the way down from my little home to Rapallo, or up from Rapallo home, I am indeed hardly conscious that this inn exists. By moonlight, too, it is negligible. Stars are rather unbecoming to it. But on a thoroughly dark night, when it is manifest as nothing but a strip of yellow light cast across the road from an ever-open door, great always is its magic for me. Is? I mean was. But then, I mean also will be. And so I cleave to the present tense—the nostalgic present, as grammarians might call it.

Likewise, when I say that thoroughly dark nights are rare here, I mean that they are rare in the Gulf of Genoa. Clouds do not seem to like our landscape. But it has often struck me that Italian nights, whenever clouds do congregate, are somehow as much darker than English nights as Italian days are brighter than days in England. They have a heavier and thicker nigritude. They shut things out from you more impenetrably. They enclose you as in a small pavilion of black velvet. This tenement is not very comfortable in a strong gale. It makes you feel rather helpless. And gales can be strong enough, in the late autumn, on the Riviera di Levante.

It is on nights when the wind blows its hardest, but makes no rift anywhere for a star to peep through, that the Golden Drugget, as I approach it, gladdens my heart the most. The distance between Rapallo and my home up yonder is rather more than two miles. The road curves and zigzags sharply, for the most part; but at the end of the first mile it runs straight for three or four hundred yards; and, as the inn stands at a point midway on this straight course, the Golden Drugget is visible to me long before I come to it. Even by starlight, it is good to see. How much better, if I happen to be out on a black rough night when nothing is disclosed but this one calm bright thing. Nothing? Well, there has been describable, all the way, a certain grey glimmer immediately in front of my feet. This, in point of fact, is the road, and by following it carefully I have managed to escape collision with trees, bushes, stone walls. The continuous shrill wailing of trees' branches writhing unseen but near, and the great hoarse roar of the sea against the rocks far down below, are no cheerful accompaniment for the buffeted pilgrim. He feels that he is engaged in single combat with Nature at her unfriendliest. He isn't sure that she hasn't supernatural allies working with her—witches on broomsticks circling closely round him, demons in pursuit of him or waiting to leap out on him. And how about mere robbers and cutthroats? Suppose—but look! that streak, yonder, look!—the Golden Drugget.

There it is, familiar, serene, festal. That the pilgrim knew he would see it in due time does not diminish for him the queer joy of seeing it; nay, this emotion would be far less without that foreknowledge. Some things are best at first sight. Others—and here is one of them—do ever improve by recognition. I remember that when first I beheld this steady strip of light, shed forth over a threshold level with the road, it seemed to me conceivably sinister. It brought Stevenson to my mind: the chink of doubloons and the clash of cutlasses; and I think I quickened pace as I passed it. But now!—now it inspires in me a sense of deep trust and gratitude; and such awe as I have for it is altogether a loving awe, as for holy ground that should he trod lightly. A drugget of crimson cloth across a London pavement is rather resented by the casual passer-by, as saying to him 'Step across me, stranger, but not along me, not in!' and for answer he spurns it with his heel. 'Stranger, come in!' is the clear message of the Golden Drugget. 'This is but a humble and earthly hostel, yet you will find here a radiant company of angels and archangels.' And always I cherish the belief that if I obeyed the summons I should receive fulfilment of the promise. Well, the beliefs that one most cherishes one is least willing to test. I do not go in at that open door. But lingering, but reluctant, is my tread as I pass by it; and I pause to bathe in the light that is as the span of our human life, granted between one great darkness and another.

HOSTS AND GUESTS

1918

Beautifully vague though the English language is, with its meanings merging into one another as softly as the facts of landscape in the moist English climate, and much addicted though we always have been to ways of compromise, and averse from sharp hard logical outlines, we do not call a host a guest, nor a guest a host. The ancient Romans did so. They, with a language that was as lucid as their climate and was a perfect expression of the sharp hard logical outlook fostered by that climate, had but one word for those two things. Nor have their equally acute descendants done what might have been expected of them in this matter. Ho^te and ospite and he'spide are as mysteriously equivocal as hospes. By weight of all this authority I find myself being dragged to the conclusion that a host and a guest must be the same thing, after all. Yet in a dim and muzzy way, deep down in my breast, I feel sure that they are different. Compromise, you see, as usual. I take it that strictly the two things are one, but that our division of them is yet another instance of that sterling common-sense by which, etc., etc.

I would go even so far as to say that the difference is more than merely circumstantial and particular. I seem to discern also a temperamental and general difference. You ask me to dine with you in a restaurant, I say I shall be delighted, you order the meal, I praise it, you pay for it, I have the pleasant sensation of not paying for it; and it is well that each of us should have a label according to the part he plays in this transaction. But the two labels are applicable in a larger and more philosophic way. In every human being one or the other of these two instincts is predominant: the active or positive instinct to offer hospitality, the negative or passive instinct to accept it. And either of these instincts is so significant of character that one might well say that mankind is divisible into two great classes: hosts and guests.

I have already (see third sentence of foregoing paragraph) somewhat prepared you for the shock of a confession which candour now forces from me. I am one of the guests. You are, however, so shocked that you will read no more of me? Bravo! Your refusal indicates that you have not a guestish soul. Here am I trying to entertain you, and you will not be entertained. You stand shouting that it is more blessed to give than to receive. Very well. For my part, I would rather read than write, any day. You shall write this essay for me. Be it never so humble, I shall give it my best attention and manage to say something nice about it. I am sorry to see you calming suddenly down. Nothing but a sense of duty to myself, and to guests in general, makes me resume my pen. I believe guests to be as numerous, really, as hosts. It may be that even you, if you examine yourself dispassionately, will find that you are one of them. In which case, you may yet thank me for some comfort. I think there are good qualities to be found in guests, and some bad ones in even the best hosts.

Our deepest instincts, bad or good, are those which we share with the rest of the animal creation. To offer hospitality, or to accept it, is but an instinct which man has acquired in the long course of his self-development. Lions do not ask one another to their lairs, nor do birds keep open nest. Certain wolves and tigers, it is true, have been so seduced by man from their natural state that they will deign to accept man's hospitality. But when you give a bone to your dog, does he run out and invite another dog to share it with him?—and does your cat insist on having a circle of other cats around her saucer of milk? Quite the contrary. A deep sense of personal property is common to all these creatures. Thousands of years hence they may have acquired some willingness to share things with their friends. Or rather, dogs may; cats, I think, not. Meanwhile, let us not be censorious. Though certain monkeys assuredly were of finer and more malleable stuff than any wolves or tigers, it was a very long time indeed before even we began to be hospitable. The cavemen did not entertain. It may be that now and again—say, towards the end of the Stone Age—one or another among the more enlightened of them said to his wife, while she plucked an eagle that he had snared the day before, 'That red-haired man who lives in the next valley seems to be a decent, harmless sort of person. And sometimes I fancy he is rather lonely. I think I will ask him to dine with us to-night,' and, presently going out, met the red-haired man and said to him, 'Are you doing anything to-night? If not, won't you dine with us? It would be a great pleasure to my wife. Only ourselves. Come just as you are.' 'That is most good of you, but,' stammered the red-haired man, 'as ill-luck will have it, I am engaged to-night. A long-standing, formal invitation. I wish I could get out of it, but I simply can't. I have a morbid conscientiousness about such things.' Thus we see that the will to offer hospitality was an earlier growth than the will to accept it. But we must beware of thinking these two things identical with the mere will to give and the mere will to receive. It is unlikely that the red-haired man would have refused a slice of eagle if it had been offered to him where he stood. And it is still more unlikely that his friend would have handed it to him. Such is not the way of hosts. The hospitable instinct is not wholly altruistic. There is pride and egoism mixed up with it, as I shall show.

Meanwhile, why did the red-haired man babble those excuses? It was because he scented danger. He was not by nature suspicious, but—what possible motive, except murder, could this man have for enticing him to that cave? Acquaintance in the open valley was all very well and pleasant, but a strange den after dark—no, no! You despise him for his fears? Yet these were not really so absurd as they may seem. As man progressed in civilisation, and grew to be definitely gregarious, hospitality became more a matter of course. But even then it was not above suspicion. It was not hedged around with those unwritten laws which make it the safe and eligible thing we know to-day. In the annals of hospitality there are many pages that make painful reading; many a great dark blot is there which the Recording Angel may wish, but will not be able, to wipe out with a tear.

If I were a host, I should ignore those tomes. Being a guest, I sometimes glance into them, but with more of horror, I assure you, than of malicious amusement. I carefully avoid those which treat of hospitality among barbarous races. Things done in the best periods of the most enlightened peoples are quite bad enough. The Israelites were the salt of the earth. But can you imagine a deed of colder-blooded treachery than Jael's? You would think it must have been held accursed by even the basest minds. Yet thus sang Deborah and Barak, 'Blessed above women shall Jael the wife of Heber the Kenite be, blessed shall she be among women in the tent.' And Barak, remember, was a gallant soldier, and Deborah was a prophetess who 'judged Israel at that time.' So much for the ideals of hospitality among the children of Israel.

Of the Homeric Greeks it may be said that they too were the salt of the earth; and it may be added that in their pungent and antiseptic quality there was mingled a measure of sweetness, not to be found in the children of Israel. I do not say outright that Odysseus ought not to have slain the suitors. That is a debatable point. It is true that they were guests under his roof. But he had not invited them. Let us give him the benefit of the doubt. I am thinking of another episode in his life. By what Circe did, and by his disregard of what she had done, a searching light is cast on the laxity of Homeric Greek notions as to what was due to guests. Odysseus was a clever, but not a bad man, and his standard of general conduct was high enough. Yet, having foiled Circe in her purpose to turn him into a swine, and having forced her to restore his comrades to human shape, he did not let pass the barrier of his teeth any such winged words as 'Now will I bide no more under thy roof, Circe, but fare across the sea with my dear comrades, even unto mine own home, for that which thou didst was an evil thing, and one not meet to be done unto strangers by the daughter of a god.' He seems to have said nothing in particular, to have accepted with alacrity the invitation that he and his dear comrades should prolong their visit, and to have prolonged it with them for a whole year, in the course of which Circe bore him a son, named Telegonus. As Matthew Arnold would have said, 'What a set!'

My eye roves, for relief, to those shelves where the later annals are. I take down a tome at random. Rome in the fifteenth century: civilisation never was more brilliant than there and then, I imagine; and yet—no, I replace that tome. I saw enough in it to remind me that the Borgias selected and laid down rare poisons in their cellars with as much thought as they gave to their vintage wines. Extraordinary!—but the Romans do not seem to have thought so. An invitation to dine at the Palazzo Borghese was accounted the highest social honour. I am aware that in recent books of Italian history there has been a tendency to whiten the Borgias' characters. But I myself hold to the old romantic black way of looking at the Borgias. I maintain that though you would often in the fifteenth century have heard the snobbish Roman say, in a would-be off-hand tone 'I am dining with the Borgias to-night,' no Roman ever was able to say 'I dined last night with the Borgias.'

To mankind in general Macbeth and Lady Macbeth stand out as the supreme type of all that a host and hostess should not be. Hence the marked coolness of Scotsmen towards Shakespeare, hence the untiring efforts of that proud and sensitive race to set up Burns in his stead. It is a risky thing to offer sympathy to the proud and sensitive, yet I must say that I think the Scots have a real grievance. The two actual, historic Macbeths were no worse than innumerable other couples in other lands that had not yet fully struggled out of barbarism. It is hard that Shakespeare happened on the story of that particular pair, and so made it immortal. But he meant no harm, and, let Scotsmen believe me, did positive good. Scotch hospitality is proverbial. As much in Scotland as in America does the English visitor blush when he thinks how perfunctory and niggard, in comparison, English hospitality is. It was Scotland that first formalised hospitality, made of it an exacting code of honour, with the basic principle that the guest must in all circumstances be respected and at all costs protected. Jacobite history bristles with examples of the heroic sacrifices made by hosts for their guests, sacrifices of their own safety and even of their own political convictions, for fear of infringing, however slightly, that sacred code of theirs. And what was the origin of all this noble pedantry? Shakespeare's 'Macbeth.'

Perhaps if England were a bleak and rugged country, like Scotland, or a new country, like America, the foreign visitor would be more overwhelmed with kindness here than he is. The landscapes of our country-side are so charming, London abounds in public monuments so redolent of history, so romantic and engrossing, that we are perhaps too apt to think the foreign visitor would have neither time nor inclination to sit dawdling in private dining-rooms. Assuredly there is no lack of hospitable impulse among the English. In what may be called mutual hospitality they touch a high level. The French, also the Italians, entertain one another far less frequently. In England the native guest has a very good time indeed—though of course he pays for it, in some measure, by acting as host too, from time to time.

In practice, no, there cannot be any absolute division of mankind into my two categories, hosts and guests. But psychologically a guest does not cease to be a guest when he gives a dinner, nor is a host not a host when he accepts one. The amount of entertaining that a guest need do is a matter wholly for his own conscience. He will soon find that he does not receive less hospitality for offering little; and he would not receive less if he offered none. The amount received by him depends wholly on the degree of his agreeableness. Pride makes an occasional host of him; but he does not shine in that capacity. Nor do hosts want him to assay it. If they accept an invitation from him, they do so only because they wish not to hurt his feelings. As guests they are fish out of water.

Circumstances do, of course, react on character. It is conventional for the rich to give, and for the poor to receive. Riches do tend to foster in you the instincts of a host, and poverty does create an atmosphere favourable to the growth of guestish instincts. But strong bents make their own way. Not all guests are to be found among the needy, nor all hosts among the affluent. For sixteen years after my education was, by courtesy, finished— from the age, that is, of twenty-two to the age of thirty-eight, I lived in London, seeing all sorts of people all the while; and I came across many a rich man who, like the master of the shepherd Corin, was 'of churlish disposition' and little recked 'to find the way to heaven by doing deeds of hospitality.' On the other hand, I knew quite poor men who were incorrigibly hospitable.

To such men, all honour. The most I dare claim for myself is that if I had been rich I should have been better than Corin's master. Even as it was, I did my best. But I had no authentic joy in doing it. Without the spur of pride I might conceivably have not done it at all. There recurs to me from among memories of my boyhood an episode that is rather significant. In my school, as in most others, we received now and again 'hampers' from home. At the mid-day dinner, in every house, we all ate together; but at breakfast and supper we ate in four or five separate 'messes.' It was customary for the receiver of a hamper to share the contents with his mess-mates. On one occasion I received, instead of the usual variegated hamper, a box containing twelve sausage-rolls. It happened that when this box arrived and was opened by me there was no one around. Of sausage-rolls I was particularly fond. I am sorry to say that I carried the box up to my cubicle, and, having eaten two of the sausage-rolls, said nothing to my friends, that day, about the other ten, nor anything about them when, three days later, I had eaten them all—all, up there, alone.

Thirty years have elapsed, my school-fellows are scattered far and wide, the chance that this page may meet the eyes of some of them does not much dismay me; but I am glad there was no collective and contemporary judgment by them on my strange exploit. What defence could I have offered? Suppose I had said 'You see, I am so essentially a guest,' the plea would have carried little weight. And yet it would not have been a worthless plea. On receipt of a hamper, a boy did rise, always, in the esteem of his mess-mates. His sardines, his marmalade, his potted meat, at any rate while they lasted, did make us think that his parents 'must be awfully decent' and that he was a not unworthy son. He had become our central figure, we expected him to lead the conversation, we liked listening to him, his jokes were good. With those twelve sausage-rolls I could have dominated my fellows for a while. But I had not a dominant nature. I never trusted myself as a leader. Leading abashed me. I was happiest in the comity of the crowd. Having received a hamper, I was always glad when it was finished, glad to fall back into the ranks. Humility is a virtue, and it is a virtue innate in guests.

Boys (as will have been surmised from my record of the effect of hampers) are all of them potential guests. It is only as they grow up that some of them harden into hosts. It is likely enough that if I, when I grew up, had been rich, my natural bent to guestship would have been diverted, and I too have become a (sort of) host. And perhaps I should have passed muster. I suppose I did pass muster whenever, in the course of my long residence in London, I did entertain friends. But the memory of those occasions is not dear to me—especially not the memory of those that were in the more distinguished restaurants. Somewhere in the back of my brain, while I tried to lead the conversation brightly, was always the haunting fear that I had not brought enough money in my pocket. I never let this fear master me. I never said to any one 'Will you have a liqueur?'—always 'What liqueur will you have?' But I postponed as far as possible the evil moment of asking for the bill. When I had, in the proper casual tone (I hope and believe), at length asked for it, I wished always it were not brought to me folded on a plate, as though the amount were so hideously high that I alone must be privy to it. So soon as it was laid beside me, I wanted to know the worst at once. But I pretended to be so occupied in talk that I was unaware of the bill's presence; and I was careful to be always in the middle of a sentence when I raised the upper fold and took my not (I hope) frozen glance. In point of fact, the amount was always much less than I had feared. Pessimism does win us great happy moments.

Meals in the restaurants of Soho tested less severely the pauper guest masquerading as host. But to them one could not ask rich persons—nor even poor persons unless one knew them very well. Soho is so uncertain that the fare is often not good enough to be palmed off on even one's poorest and oldest friends. A very magnetic host, with a great gift for bluffing, might, no doubt, even in Soho's worst moments, diffuse among his guests a conviction that all was of the best. But I never was good at bluffing. I had always to let food speak for itself. 'It's cheap' was the only paean that in Soho's bad moments ever occurred to me, and this of course I did not utter. And was it so cheap, after all? Soho induces a certain optimism. A bill there was always larger than I had thought it would be.

Every one, even the richest and most munificent of men, pays much by cheque more light-heartedly than he pays little in specie. In restaurants I should have liked always to give cheques. But in any restaurant I was so much more often seen as guest than as host that I never felt sure the proprietor would trust me. Only in my club did I know the luxury, or rather the painlessness, of entertaining by cheque. A cheque—especially if it is a club cheque, as supplied for the use of members, not a leaf torn out of his own book—makes so little mark on any man's imagination. He dashes off some words and figures, he signs his name (with that vague momentary pleasure which the sight of his own signature anywhere gives him), he walks away and forgets. Offering hospitality in my club, I was inwardly calm. But even there I did not glow (though my face and manner, I hoped, glowed). If my guest was by nature a guest, I managed to forget somewhat that I myself was a guest by nature. But if, as now and then happened, my guest was a true and habitual host, I did feel that we were in an absurdly false relation; and it was not without difficulty that I could restrain myself from saying to him 'This is all very well, you know, but—frankly: your place is at the head of your own table.'

The host as guest is far, far worse than the guest as host. He never even passes muster. The guest, in virtue of a certain hability that is part of his natural equipment, can more or less ape the ways of a host. But the host, with his more positive temperament, does not even attempt the graces of a guest. By 'graces' I do not mean to imply anything artificial. The guest's manners are, rather, as wild flowers springing from good rich soil—the soil of genuine modesty and gratitude. He honourably wishes to please in return for the pleasure he is receiving. He wonders that people should be so kind to him, and, without knowing it, is very kind to them. But the host, as I said earlier in this essay, is a guest against his own will. That is the root of the mischief. He feels that it is more blessed, etc., and that he is conferring rather than accepting a favour. He does not adjust himself. He forgets his place. He leads the conversation. He tries genially to draw you out. He never comments on the goodness of the food or wine. He looks at his watch abruptly and says he must be off. He doesn't say he has had a delightful time. In fact, his place is at the head of his own table.

His own table, over his own cellar, under his own roof—it is only there that you see him at his best. To a club or restaurant he may sometimes invite you, but not there, not there, my child, do you get the full savour of his quality. In life or literature there has been no better host than Old Wardle. Appalling though he would have been as a guest in club or restaurant, it is hardly less painful to think of him as a host there. At Dingley Dell, with an ample gesture, he made you free of all that was his. He could not have given you a club or a restaurant. Nor, when you come to think of it, did he give you Dingley Dell. The place remained his. None knew better than

Old Wardle that this was so. Hospitality, as we have agreed, is not one of the most deep-rooted instincts in man, whereas the sense of possession certainly is. Not even Old Wardle was a communist. 'This,' you may be sure he said to himself, 'is my roof, these are my horses, that's a picture of my dear old grandfather.' And 'This,' he would say to us, 'is my roof: sleep soundly under it. These are my horses: ride them. That's a portrait of my dear old grandfather: have a good look at it.' But he did not ask us to walk off with any of these things. Not even what he actually did give us would he regard as having passed out of his possession. 'That,' he would muse if we were torpid after dinner, 'is my roast beef,' and 'That,' if we staggered on the way to bed, 'is my cold milk punch.' 'But surely,' you interrupt me, 'to give and then not feel that one has given is the very best of all ways of giving.' I agree. I hope you didn't think I was trying to disparage Old Wardle. I was merely keeping my promise to point out that from among the motives of even the best hosts pride and egoism are not absent.

Every virtue, as we were taught in youth, is a mean between two extremes; and I think any virtue is the better understood by us if we glance at the vice on either side of it. I take it that the virtue of hospitality stands midway between churlishness and mere ostentation. Far to the left of the good host stands he who doesn't want to see anything of any one; far to the right, he who wants a horde of people to be always seeing something of him. I conjecture that the figure on the left, just discernible through my field-glasses, is that of old Corin's master. His name was never revealed to us, but Corin's brief account of his character suffices. 'Deeds of hospitality' is a dismal phrase that could have occurred only to the servant of a very dismal master. Not less tell-tale is Corin's idea that men who do these 'deeds' do them only to save their souls in the next world. It is a pity Shakespeare did not actually bring Corin's master on to the stage. One would have liked to see the old man genuinely touched by the charming eloquence of Rosalind's appeal for a crust of bread, and conscious that he would probably go to heaven if he granted it, and yet not quite able to grant it. Far away though he stands to the left of the good host, he has yet something in common with that third person discernible on the right—that speck yonder, which I believe to be Lucullus. Nothing that we know of Lucullus suggests that he was less inhuman than the churl of Arden. It does not appear that he had a single friend, nor that he wished for one. His lavishness was indiscriminate except in that he entertained only the rich. One would have liked to dine with him, but not even in the act of digestion could one have felt that he had a heart. One would have acknowledged that in all the material resources of his art he was a master, and also that he practised his art for sheer love of it, wishing to be admired for nothing but his mastery, and cocking no eye on any of those ulterior objects but for which some of the most prominent hosts would not entertain at all. But the very fact that he was an artist is repulsive. When hospitality becomes an art it loses its very soul. With this reflection I look away from Lucullus and, fixing my gaze on the middle ground, am the better able to appreciate the excellence of the figure that stands before me—the figure of Old Wardle. Some pride and egoism in that capacious breast, yes, but a great heart full of kindness, and ever a warm spontaneous welcome to the stranger in need, and to all old friends and young. Hark! he is shouting something. He is asking us both down to Dingley Dell. And you have shouted back that you will be delighted. Ah, did I not suspect from the first that you too were perhaps a guest?

But—I constrain you in the act of rushing off to pack your things—one moment: this essay has yet to be finished. We have yet to glance at those two extremes between which the mean is good guestship. Far to the right of the good guest, we descry the parasite; far to the left, the churl again. Not the same churl, perhaps. We do not know that Corin's master was ever sampled as a guest. I am inclined to call yonder speck Dante—Dante Alighieri, of whom we do know that he received during his exile much hospitality from many hosts and repaid them by writing how bitter was the bread in their houses, and how steep the stairs were. To think of dour Dante as a guest is less dispiriting only than to think what he would have been as a host had it ever occurred to him to entertain any one or anything except a deep regard for Beatrice; and one turns with positive relief to have a glimpse of the parasite—Mr. Smurge, I presume, 'whose gratitude was as boundless as his appetite, and his presence as unsought as it appeared to be inevitable.' But now, how gracious and admirable is the central figure—radiating gratitude, but not too much of it; never intrusive, ever within call; full of dignity, yet all amenable; quiet, yet lively; never echoing, ever amplifying; never contradicting, but often lighting the way to truth; an ornament, an inspiration, anywhere.

Such is he. But who is he? It is easier to confess a defect than to claim a quality. I have told you that when I lived in London I was nothing as a host; but I will not claim to have been a perfect guest. Nor indeed was I. I was a good one, but, looking back, I see myself not quite in the centre—slightly to the left, slightly to the churlish side. I was rather too quiet, and I did sometimes contradict. And, though I always liked to be invited anywhere, I very often preferred to stay at home. If any one hereafter shall form a collection of the notes written by me in reply to invitations, I am afraid he will gradually suppose me to have been more in request than ever I really was, and to have been also a great invalid, and a great traveller.

A POINT TO BE REMEMBERED BY
VERY EMINENT MEN

1918

One of the things a man best remembers in later years is the first time he set eyes on some illustrious elder whose achievements had already inflamed him to special reverence. In almost every autobiography you will find recorded the thrill of that first sight. With the thrill, perhaps, there was a slight shock. Great men are but life-sized. Most of them, indeed, are rather short. No matter to hero-worshipping youth. The shock did but swell the thrill. It did but enlarge the wonder that this was the man himself, the man who—

I was about to say 'who had written those inspired books.' You see, the autobiographists are usually people with an innate twist towards writing, people whose heroes, therefore, were men of letters; and thus (especially as I myself have that twist) I am apt to think of literary hero-worship as flourishing more than could any other kind. I must try to be less narrow. At first sight of the Lord Chancellor, doubtless, unforgettable emotions rise in the breast of a young man who has felt from his earliest years the passionate desire to be a lawyer. One whose dream it is to excel in trade will have been profoundly stirred at finding himself face to face with Sir Thomas Lipton. At least, I suppose so. I speak without conviction. I am inclined, after all, to think that there is in the literary temperament a special sensibility, whereby these great first envisagements mean more to it than to natures of a more practical kind. So it is primarily to men very eminent in literature that I venture to offer a hint for making those envisagements as great as possible.

The hint will serve only in certain cases. There are various ways in which a young man may chance to see his hero for the first time. 'One wintry afternoon, not long after I came to London,' the autobiographist will tell you, 'I happened to be in Cheyne Walk, bent on I know not what errand, when I saw coming slowly along the pavement an old grey-bearded man. He wore a hat of the kind that was called in those days a "wide-awake," and he leaned heavily on a stick which he carried in his right hand. I stood reverently aside to let him pass—the man who had first taught me to see, to feel, to think. Yes, it was Thomas Carlyle; and as he went by, looking neither to the right nor to the left, my heart stood still within me. What struck me most in that thought-furrowed face was the eyes. I had never, I have never since, seen a pair of eyes which,' etc., etc. This is well enough, and I don't say that the writer has exaggerated the force of the impression he received. I say merely that the impression would have been stronger still if he had seen Carlyle in a room. The open air is not really a good setting for a hero. It is too diffuse. It is too impersonal. Four walls, a ceiling, and a floor—these things are needed to concentrate for the worshipper the vision vouchsafed. Even if the room be a public one—a waiting-room, say, at Clapham Junction—it is very helpful. Far more so if it be a room in a private house, where, besides the vision itself, is thrust on the worshipper the dizzy sense of a personal relationship.

Dip with me, for an example, into some other autobiography... Here: 'Shortly after I came to London'—it is odd that autobiographists never are born or bred there—'one of the houses I found open to me was that of Mrs. T—, a woman whom (so it seemed to me when in later years I studied Italian) the word simpatica described exactly, and who, as the phrase is, "knew everybody." Calling on her one Sunday afternoon, I noticed among the guests, as I came in, a short, stalwart man with a grey beard. "I particularly," my hostess whispered to me, "want you to know Mr. Robert Browning." Everything in the room seemed to swim round me, and I had the sensation of literally sinking through the carpet when presently I found my hand held for a moment—it was only a moment, but it seemed to me an eternity—by the hand that had written "Paracelsus." I had a confused impression of something godlike about the man. His brow was magnificent. But the eyes were what stood out. Not that they were prominent eyes, but they seemed to look you through and through, and had a lustre—there is no other word for it—which,' I maintain, would have been far less dazzling out in the street, just as the world-sadness of Carlyle's eyes would have been twice as harrowing in Mrs. T—'s drawing-room.

But even there neither of those pairs of eyes could have made its fullest effect. The most terrifically gratifying way of seeing one's hero and his eyes for the first time is to see them in his own home. Anywhere else, believe me, something of his essence is forfeit. 'The rose of roses' loses more or less of its beauty in any vase, and rather more than less there in a nosegay of ordinary little blossoms (to which I rather rudely liken Mrs. T—'s other friends). The supreme flower should be first seen growing from its own Sharonian soil.

The worshipper should have, therefore, a letter of introduction. Failing that, he should write a letter introducing himself—a fervid, an idolatrous letter, not without some excuse for the writing of it: the hero's seventieth birthday, for instance, or a desire for light on some obscure point in one of his earlier works. Heroes are very human, most of them; very easily touched by praise. Some of them, however, are bad at answering letters. The worshipper must not scruple to write repeatedly, if need be. Sooner or later he will be summoned to the presence. This, perhaps, will entail a railway journey. Heroes tend to live a little way out of London. So much the better. The adventure should smack of pilgrimage. Consider also that a house in a London street cannot seem so signally its owner's own as can a house in a village or among fields. The one kind contains him, the other enshrines him, breathes of him. The sight of it, after a walk (there should be a longish walk) from the railway station, strikes great initial chords in the worshipper; and the smaller the house, the greater the chords. The worshipper pauses at the gate of the little front-garden, and when he writes his autobiography those chords will be reverberating yet. 'Here it was that the greatest of modern spirits had lived and wrought. Here in the fullness of years he abode. With I know not what tumult of thoughts I passed up the path and rang the bell. A bright-faced parlourmaid showed me into a room on the ground-floor, and said she would tell the master I was here. It was a wonderfully simple room; and something, perhaps the writing-table, told me it was his work-room, the very room from which, in the teeth of the world's neglect and misunderstanding, he had cast his spell over the minds of all thinking men and women. When I had waited a few minutes, the door opened and' after that the deluge of what was felt when the very eminent man came in.

Came in, mark you. That is a vastly important point. Had the very eminent man been there at the outset, the worshipper's first sight of him would have been a very great moment, certainly; but not nearly so great as in fact it was. Very eminent men should always, on these occasions, come in. That is the point I ask them to remember.

Honourably concerned with large high issues, they are not students of personal effect. I must therefore explain to them why it is more impressive to come into a room than to be found there.

Let those of them who have been playgoers cast their minds back to their experience of theatres. Can they recall a single play in which the principal actor was 'discovered' sitting or standing on the stage when the curtain rose? No. The actor, by the very nature of his calling, does, must, study personal effect. No playwright would dare to dump down his principal actor at the outset of a play. No sensible playwright would wish to do so. That actor's personality is a part of the playwright's material. Playwriting, it has been well said, is an art of preparing. The principal actor is one of the things for which we must be artfully prepared. Note Shakespeare's carefulness in this matter. In his day, the stage had no curtain, so that even the obscure actor who spoke the first lines (Shakespeare himself sometimes, maybe) was not ignominiously 'discovered.' But an unprepared entry is no good. The audience must first be wrought on, wrought up. Had Shakespeare been also Burbage, it is possible that he would have been even more painstaking than he was in leading up to the leading man. Assuredly, by far the most tremendous stage entries I ever saw were those of Mr. Wilson Barrett in his later days, the days when he had become his own dramatist. I remember particularly a first night of his at which I happened to be sitting next to a clever but not very successful and rather sardonic old actor. I forget just what great historic or mythic personage Mr. Barrett was to represent, but I know that the earlier scenes of the play resounded with rumours of him—accounts of the great deeds he had done, and of the yet greater deeds that were expected of him. And at length there was a procession: white-bearded priests bearing wands; maidens playing upon the sackbut; guards in full armour; a pell-mell of unofficial citizens ever prancing along the edge of the pageant, huzza-ing and hosanna-ing, mostly looking back over their shoulders and shading their eyes; maidens strewing rose-leaves; and at last the orchestra crashing to a climax in the nick of which my neighbour turned to me and, with an assumption of innocent enthusiasm, whispered, 'I shouldn't wonder if this were Barrett.' I suppose (Mr. Barrett at that instant amply appearing) I gave way to laughter; but this didn't matter; the applause would have drowned a thunderstorm, and lasted for several minutes.

My very eminent reader begins to look uncomfortable. Let him take heart. I do not want him to tamper with the simplicity of his household arrangements. Not even the one bright-faced parlourmaid need precede him with strewn petals. All the necessary preparation will have been done by the bare fact that this is his room, and that he will presently appear.

'But,' he may say, with a toss of his grey beard, 'I am not going to practise any device whatsoever. I am above devices. I shall be in the room when the young man arrives.' I assure him that I am not appealing to his vanity, merely to his good-nature. Let him remember that he too was young once, he too thrilled in harmless hero-worship. Let him not grudge the young man an utmost emotion.

Coming into a room that contains a stranger is a definite performance, a deed of which one is conscious—if one be young, and if that stranger be august. Not to come in awkwardly, not to make a bad impression, is here the paramount concern. The mind of the young man as he comes in is clogged with thoughts of self. It is free of these impediments if he shall have been waiting alone in the room. To be come in to is a thing that needs no art and induces no embarrassment. One's whole attention is focussed on the comer-in. One is the mere spectator, the passive and receptive receiver. And even supposing that the young man could come in under his hero's gaze without a thought of self, his first vision would yet lack the right intensity. A person found in a room, if it be a room strange to the arriver, does not instantly detach himself from his surroundings. He is but a feature of the scene. He does not stand out as against a background, in the grand manner of portraiture, but is fused as in an elaborately rendered 'interior.' It is all the more essential, therefore, that the worshipper shall not have his first sight of hero and room simultaneously. The room must, as it were, be an anteroom, anon converted into a presence-chamber by the hero's entry. And let not the hero be in any fear that he will bungle his entry. He has but to make it. The effect is automatic. He will stand out by merely coming in. I would but suggest that he must not, be he never so hale and hearty, bounce in. The young man must not be startled. If the mountain had come to Mahomet, it would, we may be sure, have come slowly, that the prophet should have time to realise the grandeur of the miracle. Let the hero remember that his coming, too, will seem supernatural to the young man. Let him be framed for an instant or so in the doorway—time for his eyes to produce their peculiar effect. And by the way: if he be a wearer of glasses, he should certainly remove these before coming in. He can put them on again almost immediately. It is the first moment that matters.

As to how long an interval the hero should let elapse between the young man's arrival and his own entry, I cannot offer any very exact advice. I should say, roughly, that in ten minutes the young man would be strung up to the right pitch, and that more than twenty minutes would be too much. It is important that expectancy shall have worked on him to the full, but it is still more important that his mood shall not have been chafed to impatience. The danger of over-long delay is well exemplified in the sad case of young Coventry Patmore. In his old age Patmore wrote to Mr. Gosse a description of a visit he had paid, at the age of eighteen, to Leigh Hunt; and you will find the letter on page 32, vol. I, of Mr. Basil Champneys' biography of him. The circumstances had been most propitious. The eager and sensitive spirit of the young man, his intense admiration for 'The Story of Rimini,' the letter of introduction from his father to the venerable poet and friend of greater bygone poets, the long walk to Hammersmith, the small house in a square there—all was classically in order. The poet was at home. The visitor as shown in.... 'I had,' he was destined to tell Mr. Gosse, 'waited in the little parlour at least two hours, when the door was opened and a most picturesque gentleman, with hair flowing nearly or quite to his shoulders, a beautiful velvet coat and a Vandyck collar of lace about a foot deep, appeared, rubbing his hands and smiling ethereally, and saying, without a word of preface or notice of my having waited so long, "This is a beautiful world, Mr. Patmore!" The young man was so taken aback by these words that they 'eclipsed all memory of what occurred during the remainder of the visit.'

Yet there was nothing wrong about the words themselves. Indeed, to any one with any sense of character and any knowledge of Leigh Hunt, they must seem to have been exactly, exquisitely, inevitably the right words. But they should have been said sooner.

SERVANTS

1918

It is unseemly that a man should let any ancestors of his arise from their graves to wait on his guests at table. The Chinese are a polite race, and those of them who have visited England, and gone to dine in great English houses, will not have made this remark aloud to their hosts. I believe it is only their own ancestors that they worship, so that they will not have felt themselves guilty of impiety in not rising from the table and rushing out into the night. Nevertheless, they must have been shocked.

The French Revolution, judged according to the hope it was made in, must be pronounced a failure: it effected no fundamental change in human nature. But it was by no means wholly ineffectual. For example, ladies and gentlemen ceased to powder their hair, because of it; and gentlemen adopted simpler costumes. This was so in England as well as in France. But in England ladies and gentlemen were not so nimble-witted as to be able to conceive the possibility of a world without powder. Powder had been sent down from heaven, and must not vanish from the face of the earth. Said Sir John to his Lady, "Tis a matter easy to settle. Your maid Deborah and the rest of the wenches shall powder their hair henceforth.' Whereat his Lady exclaimed in wrath, 'Lud, Sir John! Have you taken leave of your senses? A parcel of Abigails flaunting about the house in powder—oh, preposterous!' Whereat Sir John exclaimed 'Zounds!' and hotly demonstrated that since his wife had given up powder there could be no harm in its assumption by her maids. Whereat his Lady screamed and had the vapours and asked how he would like to see his own footmen flaunting about the house in powder. Whereat he (always a reasonable man, despite his hasty temper) went out and told his footmen to wear powder henceforth. And in this they obeyed him. And there arose a Lord of the Treasury, saying, 'Let powder be taxed.' And it was so, and the tax was paid, and powder was still worn. And there came the great Reform Bill, and the Steam Engine, and all manner of queer things, but powder did not end, for custom hath many lives. Nor was there an end of those things which the Nobility and Gentry had long since shed from their own persons—as, laced coats and velvet breeches and silk hose; forasmuch as without these powder could not aptly be. And it came to pass that there was a great War. And there was also a Russian Revolution, greater than the French one. And it may be that everything will be changed, fundamentally and soon. Or it may be merely that Sir John will say to his Lady, 'My dear, I have decided that the footmen shall not wear powder, and not wear livery, any more,' and that his Lady will say 'Oh, all right.' Then at length will the Eighteenth Century vanish altogether from the face of the earth.

Some of the shallower historians would have us believe that powder is deleterious to the race of footmen. They point out how plenteously footmen abounded before 1790, and how steadily their numbers have declined ever since. I do not dispute the statistics. One knows from the Table Talk of Samuel Rogers that Mr. Horne Tooke, dining tê te-a'-tê te with the first Lord Lansdowne, had counted so many as thirty footmen in attendance on the meal. That was a high figure—higher than in Rogers' day, and higher far, I doubt not, than in ours. What I refuse to believe is that the wearing of powder has caused among footmen an ever-increasing mortality. Powder was forced on them by their employers because of the French Revolution, but their subsequent fewness is traceable rather to certain ideas forced by that Revolution on their employers. The Nobility had begun to feel that it had better be just a little less noble than heretofore. When the news of the fall of the Bastille was brought to him, the first Lord Lansdowne (I conceive) remained for many hours in his study, lost in thought, and at length, rising from his chair, went out into the hall and discharged two footmen. This action may have shortened his life, but I believe it to be a fact that when he lay dying, some fifteen years later, he said to his heir, 'Discharge two more.' Such enlightenment and adaptability were not to be wondered at in so eminent a Whig. As time went on, even in the great Tory houses the number of retainers was gradually cut down. Came the Industrial Age, hailed by all publicists as the Millennium. Looms were now tended, and blast-furnaces stoked, by middle-aged men who in their youth had done nothing but hand salvers, and by young men who might have been doing just that if the Bastille had been less brittle. Noblemen, becoming less and less sure of themselves under the impact of successive Reform Bills, wished to be waited on by less and less numerous gatherings of footmen. And at length, in the course of the great War, any Nobleman not young enough to be away fighting was waited on by an old butler and a parlourmaid or two; and the ceiling did not fall.

Even if the War shall have taught us nothing else, this it will have taught us almost from its very outset: to mistrust all prophets, whether of good or of evil. Pray stone me if I predict anything at all. It may be that the War, and that remarkable by-product, the Russian Revolution, will have so worked on the minds of Noblemen that they will prefer to have not one footman in their service. Or it may be that all those men who might be footmen will prefer to earn their livelihood in other ways of life. It may even be that no more parlourmaids and housemaids, even for very illustrious houses, will be forthcoming. I do not profess to foresee. Perhaps things will go on just as before. But remember: things were going on, even then. Suppose that in the social organism generally, and in the attitude of servants particularly, the decades after the War shall bring but a gradual evolution of what was previously afoot. Even on this mild supposition must it seem likely that some of us will live to look back on domestic service, or at least on what we now mean by that term, as a curiosity of past days.

You have to look rather far behind you for the time when 'the servant question,' as it is called, had not yet begun to arise. To find servants collectively 'knowing their place,' as the phrase (not is, but) was, you have to look right back to the dawn of Queen Victoria's reign. I am not sure whether even then those Georgian notice-boards still stood in the London parks to announce that 'Ladies and Gentlemen are requested, and Servants are commanded' not to do this and that. But the spirit of those boards did still brood over the land: servants received commands, not requests, and were not 'obliging' but obedient. As for the tasks set them, I daresay the footmen in the great houses had an easy time: they were there for ornament; but the (comparatively few) maids there, and the maid or two in every home of the rapidly-increasing middle class, were very much for use, having to do an immense amount of work for a wage which would nowadays seem nominal. And they did it gladly, with no notion that they were giving much for little, or that the likes of them had any natural right to a glimpse of liberty or to a moment's more leisure than was needed to preserve their health for the benefit of their employers, or that they were not in duty bound to be truly thankful for having a roof over their devoted heads. Rare and reprehensible was the maid who, having found one roof, hankered after another. Improvident, too; for only by long and exclusive service could she hope that in her old age she would not be cast out on the parish. She might marry meanwhile? The chances were very much against that. That was an idea misbeseeming her station in life. By the rules of all households, 'followers' were fended ruthlessly away. Her state was sheer slavery? Well, she was not technically a chattel. The Law allowed her to escape at any time, after giving a month's notice; and she did not work for no wages at all, remember. This was hard on her owners? Well, in ancient Rome and elsewhere, her employers would have had to pay a large-ish sum of money for her, down, to a merchant. Economically, her employers had no genuine grievance. Her parents had handed her over to them, at a tender age, for nothing. There she was; and if she was a good girl and gave satisfaction, and if she had no gipsy strain, to make her restless for the unknown, there she ended her days, not without honour from the second or third generation of her owners. As in Ancient Rome and elsewhere, the system was, in the long run, conducive to much good feeling on either side. 'Poor Anne remained very servile in soul all her days; and was altogether occupied, from the age of fifteen to seventy-two, in doing other people's wills, not her own.' Thus wrote Ruskin, in Praeterita, of one who had been his nurse, and his father's. Perhaps the passage is somewhat marred by its first word. But Ruskin had queer views on many subjects. Besides, he was very old when, in 1885, he wrote Praeterita. Long before that date, moreover, others than he had begun to have queer views. The halcyon days were over.

Even in the 'sixties there were many dark and cumulose clouds. It was believed, however, that these would pass. 'Punch,' our ever-quick interpreter, made light of them. Absurd that Jemima Jane should imitate the bonnets of her mistress and secretly aspire to play the piano! 'Punch' and his artists, as you will find in his old volumes, were very merry about her, and no doubt his readers believed that his exquisite ridicule would kill, or his sound good sense cure, the malady in her soul. Poor misguided girl!—why was she flying in the face of Nature? Nature had decreed that some should command, others obey; that some should sit imperative all day in airy parlours, and others be executive in basements. I daresay that among the sitters aloft there were many whose indignation had a softer side to it. Under the Christian Emperors, Roman ladies were really very sorry for their slaves. It is unlikely that no English ladies were so in the 'sixties. Pity, after all, is in itself a luxury. It is for the 'some' a measure of the gulf between themselves and the 'others.' Those others had now begun to show signs of restiveness; but the gulf was as wide as ever.

Anthony Trollope was not, like 'Punch,' a mere interpreter of what was upmost in the average English mind: he was a beautifully patient and subtle demonstrator of all that was therein. Reading him, I soon forget that I am reading about fictitious characters and careers; quite soon do I feel that I am collating intimate memoirs and diaries. For sheer conviction of truth, give me Trollope. You, too, if you know him, must often have uttered this appeal. Very well. Have you been given 'Orley Farm'? And do you remember how Lady Mason felt after confessing to Sir Peregrine Orme that she had forged the will? 'As she slowly made her way across the hall, she felt that all of evil, all of punishment, had now fallen upon her. There are periods in the lives of some of us—I trust but of few—when with the silent inner voice of suffering'—and here, in justice to Trollope, I must interrupt him by saying that he seldom writes like this; and I must also, for a reason which will soon be plain, ask you not to skip a word—'we call on the mountains to fall and crush us, and on the earth to gape open and take us in—when with an agony of intensity, we wish our mothers had been barren. In these moments the poorest and most desolate are objects to us of envy, for their sufferings can be as nothing to our own. Lady Mason, as she crept silently across the hall, saw a servant girl pass down towards the entrance to the kitchen, and would have given all, all that she had in the world, to change places with that girl. But no change was possible to her. Neither would the mountains crush her, nor the earth take her in. This was her burden, and she must,' etc., etc.

You enjoyed the wondrous bathos? Of course. And yet there wasn't any bathos at all, really. At least, there wasn't any in 1862, when 'Orley Farm' was published. Servants really were 'most desolate' in those days, and 'their sufferings' were less acute only than those of gentlewomen who had forged wills. This is an exaggerated view? Well it was the view held by gentlewomen at large, in the 'sixties. Trust Trollope.

Why to a modern gentlewoman would it seem so much more dreadful to be crushed by mountains and swallowed by earthquakes than to be a servant girl passing down towards the entrance to the kitchen? In other words, how is it that servants have so much less unpleasant a time than they were having half-a-century ago? I should like to think this melioration came through our sense of justice, but I cannot claim that it did. Somehow, our sense of justice never turns in its sleep till long after the sense of injustice in others has been thoroughly aroused; nor is it ever up and doing till those others have begun to make themselves thoroughly disagreeable, and not even then will it be up and doing more than is urgently required of it by our convenience at the moment. For the improvement in their lot, servants must, I am afraid, be allowed to thank themselves rather than their employers. I am not going to trace the stages of that improvement. I will not try to decide in what year servants passed from wistfulness to resentment, or from resentment to exaction. This is not a sociological treatise, it is just an essay; and I claim an essayist's privilege of not groping through the library of the British Museum on the chance of mastering all the details. I confess that I did go there yesterday, thinking I should find in Mr. and Mrs. Sidney Webb's 'History of Trade Unionism' the means of appearing to know much. But I drew blank. It would seem that servants have no trade union. This is strange. One would not have thought so much could be done without organisation. The mere Spirit of the Time, sneaking down the steps of areas, has worked wonders. There has been no servants' campaign, no strategy, nothing but an infinite series of spontaneous and sporadic little risings in isolated households. Wonders have been worked, yes. But servants are not yet satiated with triumph. More and more, on the contrary, do they glide—long before the War they had begun gliding—away into other forms of employment. Not merely are the changed conditions of domestic service not changed enough for them: they seem to despise the thing itself. It was all very well so long as they had not been taught to read and write, but—There, no doubt, is the root of the mischief. Had the governing classes not forced those accomplishments on them in 1872— But there is no use in repining. What's done can't be undone. On the other hand, what must be done can't be left undone. Housework, for example. What concessions by the governing classes, what bribes, will be big enough hereafter to get that done?

Perhaps the governing classes will do it for themselves, eventually, and their ceilings not fall. Or perhaps there will be no more governing classes—merely the State and its swarms of neat little overseers, male and female. I know not whether in this case the sum of human happiness will be greater, but it will certainly—it and the sum of human dullness—be more evenly distributed. I take it that under any scheme of industrial compulsion for the young a certain number of the conscripts would be told off for domestic service. To every family in every flat (houses not legal) would be assigned one female member of the community. She would be twenty years old, having just finished her course of general education at a municipal college. Three years would be her term of industrial (sub-sect. domestic) service. Her diet, her costume, her hours of work and leisure, would be standardised, but the lenses of her pince-nez would be in strict accordance to her own eyesight. If her employers found her faulty in work or conduct, and proved to the visiting inspector that she was so, she would be penalised by an additional term of service. If she, on the other hand, made good any complaint against her employers, she would be transferred to another flat, and they be penalised by suspension of their license to employ. There would always be chances of friction. But these chances would not be so numerous nor so great as they are under that lack of system which survives to-day.

Servants would be persons knowing that for a certain period certain tasks were imposed on them, tasks tantamount to those in which all their coevals were simultaneously engaged. To-day they are persons not knowing, as who should say, where they are, and wishing all the while they were elsewhere—and mostly, as I have said, going elsewhere. Those who remain grow more and more touchy, knowing themselves a mock to the rest; and their qualms, even more uncomfortably than their demands and defects, are always haunting their employers. It seems almost incredible that there was a time when Mrs. Smith said 'Sarah, your master wishes—' or Mr. Smith said 'Sarah, go up and ask your mistress whether—' I am well aware that the very title of this essay jars. I wish I could find another; but in writing one must be more explicit than one need be by word of mouth. I am well aware that the survival of domestic service, in its old form, depends more and more on our agreement not to mention it.

Assuredly, a most uncomfortable state of things. Is it, after all, worth saving?—a form so depleted of right human substance, an anomaly so ticklish. Consider, in your friend's house, the cheerful smile of yonder parlourmaid; hark to the housemaid's light brisk tread in the corridor; note well the slight droop of the footman's shoulders as he noiselessly draws near. Such things, as being traditional, may pander to your sense of the great past. Histrionically, too, they are good. But do you really like them? Do they not make your blood run a trifle cold? In the thick of the great past, you would have liked them well enough, no doubt. I myself am old enough to have known two or three servants of the old school—later editions of Ruskin's Anne. With them there was no discomfort, for they had no misgiving. They had never wished (heaven help them!) for more, and in the process of the long years had acquired, for inspiration of others, much—a fine mellowness, the peculiar sort of dignity, even of wisdom, that comes only of staying always in the same place, among the same people, doing the same things perpetually. Theirs was the sap that rises only from deep roots, and where they were you had always the sense of standing under great wide branches. One especially would I recall, who—no, personally I admire the plungingly intimate kind of essayist very much indeed, but I never was of that kind, and it's too late to begin now. For a type of old-world servant I would recall rather some more public worthy, such as that stout old hostler whom, whenever you went up to stay in Hampstead, you would see standing planted outside that stout old hostelry, Jack Straw's Castle. He stands there no more, and the hostelry can never again be to me all that it was of solid comfort. Or perhaps, as he was so entirely an outside figure, I might rather say that Hampstead itself is not what it was. His robust but restful form, topped with that weather-beaten and chin-bearded face, was the hub of the summit of Hampstead. He was as richly local as the pond there—that famous pond which in hot weather is so much waded through by cart-horses and is at all seasons so much barked around by excitable dogs and cruised on by toy boats. He was as essential as it and the flag-staff and the gorse and the view over the valley away to Highgate. It was always to Highgate that his big blue eyes were looking, and on Highgate that he seemed to be ruminating. Not that I think he wanted to go there. He was Hampstead-born and Hampstead-bred, and very loyal to that village. In the course of his life he had 'bin down to London a matter o' three or four times,' he would tell me, 'an' slep' there once.' He knew me to be a native of that city, and, for he was the most respectful of men, did not make any adverse criticism of it. But clearly it had not prepossessed him. Men and—horses rather than cities were what he knew. And his memory was more retentive of horses than of men. But he did—and this was a great thrill for me—did, after some pondering at my behest, remember to have seen in Heath Street, when he was a boy, 'a gen'leman with summut long hair, settin' in a small cart, takin' a pictur'.' To me Ford Madox Brown's 'Work' is of all modern pictur's the most delightful in composition and strongest in conception, the most alive and the most worth-while; and I take great pride in having known some one who saw it in the making. But my friend himself set little store on anything that had befallen him in days before he was 'took on as stable-lad at the Castle.' His pride was in the Castle, wholly.

Part of his charm, like Hampstead's, was in the surprise one had at finding anything like it so near to London. Even now, if you go to districts near which no great towns are, you will find here and there an inn that has a devoted waiter, a house with a fond butler. As to butlers elsewhere, butlers in general, there is one thing about them that I do not at all understand. It seems to be against nature, yet it is a fact, that in the past forty years they have been growing younger; and slimmer. In my childhood they were old, without exception; and stout. At the close of the last century they had gradually relapsed into middle age, losing weight all the time. And in the years that followed they were passing back behind the prime of life, becoming willowy juveniles. In 1915, it is true, the work of past decades was undone butlers: were suddenly as old and stout as ever they were, and so they still are. But this, I take it, is only a temporary setback. At the restoration of peace butlers will reappear among us as they were in 1915, and anon will be losing height and weight too, till they shall have become bright-eyed children, with pattering feet. Or will their childhood be of a less gracious kind than that? I fear so. I have seen, from time to time, butlers who had shed all semblance of grace, butlers whose whole demeanour was a manifesto of contempt for their calling and of devotion to the Spirit of the Age. I have seen a butler in a well-established household strolling around the diners without the slightest droop, and pouring out wine in an off-hand and quite obviously hostile manner. I have seen him, towards the end of the meal, yawning. I remember another whom, positively, I heard humming—a faint sound indeed, but menacing as the roll of tumbrils.

These were exceptional cases, I grant. For the most part, the butlers observed by me have had a manner as correctly smooth and colourless as their very shirt-fronts. Aye, and in two or three of them, modern though they were in date and aspect, I could have sworn there was 'a flame of old-world fealty all bright.' Were these but the finer comedians? There was one (I will call him Brett) who had an almost dog-like way of watching his master. Was this but a calculated touch in a merely aesthetic whole? Brett was tall and slender, and his movements were those of a greyhound under perfect self-control. Baldness at the temples enhanced the solemnity of his thin smooth face. It is more than twenty years since first I saw him; and for a long period I saw him often, both in town and in country. Against the background of either house he was impeccable. Many butlers might be that. Brett's supremacy was in the sense he gave one that he was, after all, human—that he had a heart, in which he had taken the liberty to reserve a corner for any true friend of his master and mistress. I remember well the first time he overstepped sheer formality in relation to myself. It was one morning in the country, when my entertainers and my fellow guests had gone out in pursuit of some sport at which I was no good. I was in the smoking room, reading a book. Suddenly—no, Brett never appeared anywhere suddenly. Brett appeared, paused at precisely the right speaking distance, and said in a low voice, 'I thought it might interest you to know, sir, that there's a white-tailed magpie out on the lawn. Very rare, as you know, sir. If you look out of the window you will see the little fellow hopping about on the lawn.' I thanked him effusively as I darted to the window, and simulated an intense interest in 'the little fellow.' I greatly overdid my part. Exit Brett, having done his to perfection.

What worries me is not that I showed so little self-command and so much insincerity, but the doubt whether Brett's flawless technique was the vehicle for an act of true good feeling or was used simply for the pleasure of using it. Similar doubts abide in all my special memories of him. There was an evening when he seemed to lose control over himself—but did he really lose it? There were only four people at dinner: my host, his wife, their nephew (a young man famous for drollery), and myself. Towards the end of dinner the conversation had turned on early marriages. 'I,' said the young man presently, 'shall not marry till I am seventy. I shall then marry some charming girl of seventeen.' His aunt threw up her hands, exclaiming, 'Oh, Tom, what a perfectly horrible idea! Why, she isn't born yet!' 'No,' said the young man, 'but I have my eye on her mother.' At this, Brett, who was holding a light for his master's cigarette, turned away convulsively, with a sudden dip of the head, and vanished from the room. His breakdown touched and pleased all four beholders. But—was it a genuine lapse? Or merely a feint to thrill us?—the feint of an equilibrist so secure that he can pretend to lose his balance?

If I knew why Brett ceased to be butler in that household, I might be in less doubt as to the true inwardness of him. I knew only that he was gone. That was fully ten years ago. Since then I have had one glimpse of him. This was on a summer night in London. I had gone out late to visit some relatives and assure myself that they were safe and sound; for Zeppelins had just passed over London for the first time. Not so much horror as a very deep disgust was the atmosphere in the populous quiet streets and squares. One square was less quiet than others, because somebody was steadily whistling for a taxi. Anon I saw the whistler silhouetted in the light cast out on a wide doorstep from an open door, and I saw that he was Brett. His attitude, as he bent out into the dark night, was perfect in grace, but eloquent of a great tensity—even of agony. Behind him stood a lady in an elaborate evening cloak. Brett's back must have conveyed to her in every curve his surprise, his shame, that she should be kept waiting. His chivalry in her behalf was such as Burke's for Marie Antoinette—little had he dreamed that he should have lived to see such disasters fallen upon her in a nation of gallant men, in a nation of men of honour, and of cavaliers. He had thought ten thousand taxis must have leaped from their stands, etc. The whistle that at first sounded merely mechanical and ear-piercing had become heartrending and human when I saw from whom it proceeded—a very heart-cry that still haunts me. But was it a heart-cry? Was Brett, is Brett more than a mere virtuoso?

He is in any case what employers call a treasure, and to any one who wishes to go forth and hunt for him I will supply a chart showing the way to that doorstep on which last I saw him. But I myself, were I ever so able to pay his wages, should never covet him—no, nor anything like him. Perhaps we are not afraid of menservants if we look out at them from the cradle. None was visible from mine. Only in later years and under external auspices did I come across any of them. And I am as afraid of them as ever. Maidservants frighten me less, but they also—except the two or three ancients aforesaid—have always struck some degree of terror to my soul. The whole notion of domestic service has never not seemed to me unnatural. I take no credit for enlightenment. Not to have the instinct to command implies a lack of the instinct to obey. The two aptitudes are but different facets of one jewel: the sense of order. When I became a schoolboy, I greatly disliked being a monitor's fag. Other fags there were who took pride in the quality of the toast they made for the breakfasts and suppers of their superiors. My own feeling was that I would rather eat it myself, and that if I mightn't eat it myself I would rather it were not very good. Similarly, when I grew to have fags of my own, and by morning and by evening one of them solemnly entered to me bearing a plate on which those three traditional pieces of toast were solemnly propped one against another, I cared not at all whether the toast were good or bad, having no relish for it at best, but could have eaten with gusto toast made by my own hand, not at all understanding why that member should be accounted too august for such employment. Even so in my later life. Loth to obey, loth to command. Convention (for she too frightens me) has made me accept what servants would do for me by rote. But I would liefer have it ill-done than ask even the least mettlesome of them to do it better, and far liefer, if they would only be off and not do it at all, do it for myself. In Italy—dear Italy, where I have lived much—servants do still regard service somewhat in the old way, as a sort of privilege; so that with Italian servants I am comparatively at my ease. But oh, the delight when on the afternoon of some local festa there is no servant at all in the little house! Oh, the reaction, the impulse to sing and dance, and the positive quick obedience to that impulse! Convention alone has forced me to be anywhere a master. Ariel and Caliban, had I been Prospero on that island, would have had nothing to do and nothing to complain of; and Man Friday on that other island would have bored me, had I been Crusoe. When I was a king in Babylon and you were a Christian slave, I promptly freed you.

Anarchistic? Yes; and I have no defence to offer, except the rather lame one that I am a Tory Anarchist. I should like every one to go about doing just as he pleased—short of altering any of the things to which I have grown accustomed. Domestic service is not one of those things, and I should be glad were there no more of it.

GOING OUT FOR A WALK

1918

It is a fact that not once in all my life have I gone out for a walk. I have been taken out for walks; but that is another matter. Even while I trotted prattling by my nurse's side I regretted the good old days when I had, and wasn't, a perambulator. When I grew up it seemed to me that the one advantage of living in London was that nobody ever wanted me to come out for a walk. London's very drawbacks—its endless noise and hustle, its smoky air, the squalor ambushed everywhere in it—assured this one immunity. Whenever I was with friends in the country, I knew that at any moment, unless rain were actually falling, some man might suddenly say 'Come out for a walk!' in that sharp imperative tone which he would not dream of using in any other connexion. People seem to think there is something inherently noble and virtuous in the desire to go for a walk. Any one thus desirous feels that he has a right to impose his will on whomever he sees comfortably settled in an arm-chair, reading. It is easy to say simply 'No' to an old friend. In the case of a mere acquaintance one wants some excuse. 'I wish I could, but'—nothing ever occurs to me except 'I have some letters to write.' This formula is unsatisfactory in three ways. (1) It isn't believed. (2) It compels you to rise from your chair, go to the writing-table, and sit improvising a letter to somebody until the walkmonger (just not daring to call you liar and hypocrite) shall have lumbered out of the room. (3) It won't operate on Sunday mornings. 'There's no post out till this evening' clinches the matter; and you may as well go quietly.

Walking for walking's sake may be as highly laudable and exemplary a thing as it is held to be by those who practise it. My objection to it is that it stops the brain. Many a man has professed to me that his brain never works so well as when he is swinging along the high road or over hill and dale. This boast is not confirmed by my memory of anybody who on a Sunday morning has forced me to partake of his adventure. Experience teaches me that whatever a fellow-guest may have of power to instruct or to amuse when he is sitting on a chair, or standing on a hearth-rug, quickly leaves him when he takes one out for a walk. The ideas that came so thick and fast to him in any room, where are they now? where that encyclopiedic knowledge which he bore so lightly? where the kindling fancy that played like summer lightning over any topic that was started? The man's face that was so mobile is set now; gone is the light from his fine eyes. He says that A. (our host) is a thoroughly good fellow. Fifty yards further on, he adds that A. is one of the best fellows he has ever met. We tramp another furlong or so, and he says that Mrs. A. is a charming woman. Presently he adds that she is one of the most charming women he has ever known. We pass an inn. He reads vapidly aloud to me: 'The King's Arms. Licensed to sell Ales and Spirits.' I foresee that during the rest of the walk he will read aloud any inscription that occurs. We pass a milestone. He points at it with his stick, and says 'Uxminster. 11 Miles.' We turn a sharp corner at the foot of a hill. He points at the wall, and says 'Drive Slowly.' I see far ahead, on the other side of the hedge bordering the high road, a small notice-board. He sees it too. He keeps his eye on it. And in due course 'Trespassers,' he says, 'Will Be Prosecuted.' Poor man!—mentally a wreck.

Luncheon at the A.s, however, salves him and floats him in full sail. Behold him once more the life and soul of the party. Surely he will never, after the bitter lesson of this morning, go out for another walk. An hour later, I see him striding forth, with a new companion. I watch him out of sight. I know what he is saying. He is saying that I am rather a dull man to go a walk with. He will presently add that I am one of the dullest men he ever went a walk with. Then he will devote himself to reading out the inscriptions.

How comes it, this immediate deterioration in those who go walking for walking's sake? Just what happens? I take it that not by his reasoning faculties is a man urged to this enterprise. He is urged, evidently, by something in him that transcends reason; by his soul, I presume. Yes, it must be the soul that raps out the 'Quick march!' to the body.— 'Halt! Stand at ease!' interposes the brain, and 'To what destination,' it suavely asks the soul, 'and on what errand, are you sending the body?'—'On no errand whatsoever,' the soul makes answer, 'and to no destination at all. It is just like you to be always on the look-out for some subtle ulterior motive. The body is going out because the mere fact of its doing so is a sure indication of nobility, probity, and rugged grandeur of character.'—'Very well, Vagula, have your own wayula! But I,' says the brain, 'flatly refuse to be mixed up in this tomfoolery. I shall go to sleep till it is over.' The brain then wraps itself up in its own convolutions, and falls into a dreamless slumber from which nothing can rouse it till the body has been safely deposited indoors again.

Even if you go to some definite place, for some definite purpose, the brain would rather you took a vehicle; but it does not make a point of this; it will serve you well enough unless you are going for a walk. It won't, while your legs are vying with each other, do any deep thinking for you, nor even any close thinking; but it will do any number of small odd jobs for you willingly—provided that your legs, also, are making themselves useful, not merely bandying you about to gratify the pride of the soul. Such as it is, this essay was composed in the course of a walk, this morning. I am not one of those extremists who must have a vehicle to every destination. I never go out of my way, as it were, to avoid exercise. I take it as it comes, and take it in good part. That valetudinarians are always chattering about it, and indulging in it to excess, is no reason for despising it. I am inclined to think that in moderation it is rather good for one, physically. But, pending a time when no people wish me to go and see them, and I have no wish to go and see any one, and there is nothing whatever for me to do off my own premises, I never will go out for a walk.

QUIA IMPERFECTUM

1918

I have often wondered that no one has set himself to collect unfinished works of art. There is a peculiar charm for all of us in that which was still in the making when its maker died, or in that which he laid aside because he was tired of it, or didn't see his way to the end of it, or wanted to go on to something else. Mr. Pickwick and the Ancient Mariner are valued friends of ours, but they do not preoccupy us like Edwin Drood or Kubla Khan. Had that revolving chair at Gad's Hill become empty but a few weeks later than it actually did, or had Samuel Taylor Coleridge in the act of setting down his dream about the Eastern potentate not been interrupted by 'a person on business from Porlock' and so lost the thread of the thing for ever, from two what delightful glades for roaming in would our fancy be excluded! The very globe we live on is a far more fascinating sphere than it can have been when men supposed that men like themselves would be on it to the end of time. It is only since we heard what Darwin had to say, only since we have had to accept as improvisible what lies far ahead, that the Book of Life has taken so strong a hold on us and 'once taken up, cannot,' as the reviewers say, 'readily be laid down.' The work doesn't strike us as a masterpiece yet, certainly; but who knows that it isn't—that it won't be, judged as a whole?

For sheer creativeness, no human artist, I take it, has a higher repute than Michael Angelo; none perhaps has a repute so high. But what if Michael Angelo had been a little more persevering? All those years he spent in the process of just a-going to begin Pope Julius' tomb, and again, all those blank spaces for his pictures and bare pedestals for his statues in the Baptistery of San Lorenzo—ought we to regret them quite so passionately as we do? His patrons were apt to think him an impossible person to deal with. But I suspect that there may have been a certain high cunning in what appeared to be a mere lovable fault of temperament. When Michael Angelo actually did bring a thing off, the result was not always more than magnificent. His David is magnificent, but it isn't David. One is duly awed, but, to see the master at his best, back one goes from the Accademia to that marvellous bleak Baptistery which he left that we should see, in the mind's eye, just that very best.

It was there, some years ago, as I stood before the half-done marvel of the Night and Morning, that I first conceived the idea of a museum of incomplete masterpieces. And now I mean to organise the thing on my own account. The Baptistery itself, so full of unfulfilment, and with such a wealth, at present, of spare space, will be the ideal setting for my treasures. There be it that the public shall throng to steep itself in the splendour of possibilities, beholding, under glass, and perhaps in excellent preservation, Penelope's web and the original designs for the Tower of Babel, the draft made by Mr. Asquith for a reformed House of Lords and the notes jotted down by the sometime German Emperor for a proclamation from Versailles to the citizens of Paris. There too shall be the MS. of that fragmentary 'Iphige'nie' which Racine laid aside so meekly at the behest of Mlle. de Tre'ves—'quoique cela fu^t de mon mieux'; and there an early score of that one unfinished Symphony of Beethoven's—I forget the number of it, but anyhow it is my favourite. Among the pictures, Rossetti's oil-painting of 'Found' must be ruled out, because we know by more than one drawing just what it would have been, and how much less good than those drawings. But Leonardo's St. Sebastian (even if it isn't Leonardo's) shall be there, and Whistler's Miss Connie Gilchrist, and numerous other pictures that I would mention if my mind were not so full of one picture to which, if I can find it and acquire it, a special place of honour shall be given: a certain huge picture in which a life-sized gentleman, draped in a white mantle, sits on a fallen obelisk and surveys the ruined temples of the Campagna Romana.

The reader knits his brow? Evidently he has not just been reading Goethe's 'Travels in Italy.' I have. Or rather, I have just been reading a translation of it, published in 1885 by George Bell & Sons. I daresay it isn't a very good translation (for one has always understood that Goethe, despite a resistant medium, wrote well—an accomplishment which this translator hardly wins one to suspect). And I daresay the painting I so want to see and have isn't a very good painting. Wilhelm Tischbein is hardly a name to conjure with, though in his day, as a practitioner in the 'historical' style, and as a rapturous resident in Rome, Tischbein did great things; big things, at any rate. He did crowds of heroes in helmets looked down at by gods on clouds; he did centaurs leaping ravines; Sabine women; sieges of Troy. And he did this portrait of Goethe. At least he began it. Why didn't he finish it? That is a problem as to which one can but hazard guesses, reading between the lines of Goethe's letters. The great point is that it never was finished. By that point, as you read between those lines, you will be amused if you are unkind, and worried if you are humane.

Worried, yet also pleased. Goethe has more than once been described as 'the perfect man.' He was assuredly a personage on the great scale, in the grand manner, gloriously balanced, rounded. And it is a fact that he was not made of marble. He started with all the disadvantages of flesh and blood, and retained them to the last. Yet from no angle, as he went his long way, could it be plausibly hinted that he wasn't sublime. Endearing though failure always is, we grudge no man a moderately successful career, and glory itself we will wink at if it befall some thoroughly good fellow. But a man whose career was glorious without intermission, decade after decade, does sorely try our patience. He, we know, cannot have been a thoroughly good fellow. Of Goethe we are shy for such reasons as that he was never injudicious, never lazy, always in his best form—and always in love with some lady or another just so much as was good for the development of his soul and his art, but never more than that by a tittle. Fate decreed that Sir Willoughby Patterne should cut a ridiculous figure and so earn our forgiveness. Fate may have had a similar plan for Goethe; if so, it went all agley. Yet, in the course of that pageant, his career, there did happen just one humiliation—one thing that needed to be hushed up. There Tischbein's defalcation was; a chip in the marble, a flaw in the crystal, just one thread loose in the great grand tapestry.

Men of genius are not quick judges of character. Deep thinking and high imagining blunt that trivial instinct by which you and I size people up. Had you and I been at Goethe's elbow when, in the October of 1786, he entered Rome and was received by the excited Tischbein, no doubt we should have whispered in his ear, 'Beware of that man! He will one day fail you.' Unassisted Goethe had no misgivings. For some years he had been receiving letters from this Herr Tischbein. They were the letters of a man steeped in the Sorrows of Werther and in all else that Goethe had written. This was a matter of course. But also they were the letters of a man familiar with all the treasures of Rome. All Italy was desirable; but it was especially towards great Rome that the soul of the illustrious poet, the confined State Councillor of Weimar, had been ever yearning. So that when came the longed-for day, and the Duke gave leave of absence, and Goethe, closing his official portfolio with a snap and imprinting a fervent but hasty kiss on the hand of Frau von Stein, fared forth on his pilgrimage, Tischbein was a prospect inseparably bound up for him with that of the Seven Hills. Baedeker had not been born. Tischbein would be a great saviour of time and trouble. Nor was this hope unfulfilled. Tischbein was assiduous, enthusiastic, indefatigable. In the early letters to Frau von Stein, to Herder and others, his name is always cropping up for commendation. 'Of Tischbein I have much to say and much to boast'—'A thorough and original

German'—'He has always been thinking of me, ever providing for my wants'—'In his society all my enjoyments are more than doubled.' He was thirty-five years old (two years younger than Goethe), and one guesses him to have been a stocky little man, with those short thick legs which denote indefatigability. One guesses him blond and rosy, very voluble, very guttural, with a wealth of forceful but not graceful gesture.

One is on safer ground in guessing him vastly proud of trotting Goethe round. Such fame throughout Europe had Goethe won by his works that it was necessary for him to travel incognito. Not that his identity wasn't an open secret, nor that he himself would have wished it hid. Great artists are always vain. To say that a man is vain means merely that he is pleased with the effect he produces on other people. A conceited man is satisfied with the effect he produces on himself. Any great artist is far too perceptive and too exigent to be satisfied with that effect, and hence in vanity he seeks solace. Goethe, you may be sure, enjoyed the hero-worshipful gaze focussed on him from all the tables of the Caffe' Greco. But not for adulation had he come to Rome. Rome was what he had come for; and the fussers of the coteries must not pester him in his golden preoccupation with the antique world. Tischbein was very useful in warding off the profane throng—fanning away the flies. Let us hope he was actuated solely by zeal in Goethe's interest, not by the desire to swagger as a monopolist.

Clear it is, though, that he scented fine opportunities in Goethe's relation to him. Suppose he could rope his illustrious friend in as a collaborator! He had begun a series of paintings on the theme of primaeval man. Goethe was much impressed by these. Tischbein suggested a great poem on the theme of primaeval man—a volume of engravings after Tischbein, with running poetic commentary by Goethe. 'Indeed, the frontispiece for such a joint work,' writes Goethe in one of his letters, 'is already designed.' Pushful Tischbein! But Goethe, though he was the most courteous of men, was not of the stuff of which collaborators are made. 'During our walks together'—and can you not see those two together, pacing up and down the groves of the Villa Pamphili, or around the ruins of the Temple of Jupiter?—little Tischbein gesticulating and peering up into Goethe's face, and Goethe with his hands clasped behind him, ever nodding in a non-committal manner—'he has talked with me in the hope of gaining me over to his views, and getting me to enter upon the plan.' Goethe admits in another letter that 'the idea is beautiful; only,' he adds, 'the artist and the poet must be many years together, in order to carry out and execute such a work'; and one conceives that he felt a certain lack of beauty in the idea of being with Tischbein for many years. 'Did I not fear to enter upon any new tasks at present, I might perhaps be tempted.' This I take to be but the repetition of a formula often used in the course of those walks. In no letter later than November is the scheme mentioned. Tischbein had evidently ceased to press it. Anon he fell back on a scheme less glorious but likelier to bear fruit.

'Latterly,' writes Goethe, 'I have observed Tischbein regarding me; and now'—note the demure pride!— 'it appears that he has long cherished the idea of painting my portrait.' Earnest sight-seer though he was, and hard at work on various MSS. in the intervals of sight-seeing, it is evident that to sit for his portrait was a new task which he did not 'fear to enter upon at present.' Nor need we be surprised. It seems to be a law of nature that no man, unless he has some obvious physical deformity, e-ver is loth to sit for his portrait. A man may be old, he may be ugly, he may be burdened with grave responsibilities to the nation, and that nation be at a crisis of its history; but none of these considerations, nor all of them together, will deter him from sitting for his portrait. Depend on him to arrive at the studio punctually, to surrender himself and sit as still as a mouse, trying to look his best in whatever posture the painter shall have selected as characteristic, and talking (if he have leave to talk) with a touching humility and with a keen sense of his privilege in being allowed to pick up a few ideas about art. To a dentist or a hairdresser he surrenders himself without enthusiasm, even with resentment. But in the atmosphere of a studio there is something that entrances him. Perhaps it is the smell of turpentine that goes to his head. Or more likely it is the idea of immortality. Goethe was one of the handsomest men of his day, and (remember) vain, and now in the prime of life; so that he was specially susceptible to the notion of being immortalised. 'The design is already settled, and the canvas stretched'; and I have no doubt that in the original German these words ring like the opening of a ballad. 'The anchor's up and the sail is spread,' as I (and you, belike) recited in childhood. The ship in that poem foundered, if I remember rightly; so that the analogy to Goethe's words is all the more striking.

It is in this same letter that the poet mentions those three great points which I have already laid before you: the fallen obelisk for him to sit on, the white mantle to drape him, and the ruined temples for him to look at. 'It will form a beautiful piece, but,' he sadly calculates, 'it will be rather too big for our northern habitations.' Courage! There will be plenty of room for it in the Baptistery of San Lorenzo.

Meanwhile, the work progressed. A brief visit to Naples and Sicily was part of Goethe's well-pondered campaign, and he was to set forth from Rome (taking Tischbein with him) immediately after the close of the Carnival—but not a moment before. Needless to say, he had no idea of flinging himself into the Carnival, after the fashion of lesser and lighter tourists. But the Carnival was a great phenomenon to be studied. All-embracing Goethe, remember, was nearly as keen on science as on art. He had ever been patient in poring over plants botanically, and fishes ichthyologically, and minerals mineralogically. And now, day by day, he studied the Carnival from a strictly carnivalogical standpoint, taking notes on which he founded later a classic treatise. His presence was not needed in the studio during these days, for the life-sized portrait 'begins already to stand out from the canvas,' and Tischbein was now painting the folds of the mantle, which were swathed around a clay figure. 'He is working away diligently, for the work must, he says, be brought to a certain point before we start for Naples.' Besides the mantle, Tischbein was doing the Campagna. I remember that some years ago an acquaintance of mine, a painter who was neither successful nor talented, but always buoyant, told me he was starting for Italy next day. 'I am going,' he said, 'to paint the Campagna. The Campagna WANTS painting.' Tischbein was evidently giving it a good dose of what it wanted. 'It takes no little time,' writes Goethe to Frau von Stein, 'merely to cover so large a field of canvas with colours.

Ash Wednesday ushered itself in, and ushered the Carnival out. The curtain falls, rising a few days later on the Bay of Naples. Re-enter Goethe and Tischbein. Bright blue backcloth. Incidental music of barcaroles, etc. For a while, all goes splendidly well. Sane Quixote and aesthetic Sancho visit the churches, the museums; visit Pompeii; visit our Ambassador, Sir William Hamilton, that accomplished man. Vesuvius is visited too; thrice by Goethe, but (here, for the first time, we feel a vague uneasiness) only once by Tischbein. To Goethe, as you may well imagine, Vesuvius was strongly attractive. At his every ascent he was very brave, going as near as possible to the crater, which he approached very much as he had approached the Carnival, not with any wish to fling himself into it, but as a resolute scientific inquirer. Tischbein, on the other hand, merely disliked and feared Vesuvius. He said it had no aesthetic value, and at his one ascent did not accompany Goethe to the crater's edge. He seems to have regarded Goethe's bravery as rashness. Here, you see, is a rift, ever so slight, but of evil omen; what seismologists call 'a fault.'

Goethe was unconscious of its warning. Throughout his sojourn in Naples he seems to have thought that Tischbein in Naples was the same as Tischbein in Rome. Of some persons it is true that change of sky works no change of soul. Oddly enough, Goethe reckoned himself among the changeable. In one of his letters he calls himself 'quite an altered man,' and asserts that he is given over to 'a sort of intoxicated self-forgetfulness'—a condition to which his letters testify not at all. In a later bulletin he is nearer the mark: 'Were I not impelled by the German spirit, and desire to learn and do rather than to enjoy, I should tarry a little longer in this school of a light-hearted and happy life, and try to profit by it still more.' A truly priceless passage, this, with a solemnity transcending logic—as who should say, 'Were I not so thoroughly German, I should be thoroughly German.' Tischbein was of less stern stuff, and it is clear that Naples fostered in him a lightness which Rome had repressed. Goethe says that he himself puzzled the people in Neapolitan society: 'Tischbein pleases them far better. This evening he hastily painted some heads of the size of life, and about these they disported themselves as strangely as the New Zealanders at the sight of a ship of war.' One feels that but for Goethe's presence Tischbein would have cut New Zealand capers too. A week later he did an utterly astounding thing. He told Goethe that he would not be accompanying him to Sicily.

He did not, of course, say 'The novelty of your greatness has worn off. Your solemnity oppresses me. Be off, and leave me to enjoy myself in Naples-on-Sea—Naples, the Queen of Watering Places!' He spoke of work which he had undertaken, and recommended as travelling companion for Goethe a young man of the name of Kniep.

Goethe, we may be sure, was restrained by pride from any show of wrath. Pride compelled him to make light of the matter in his epistles to the Weimarians. Even Kniep he accepted with a good grace, though not without misgivings. He needed a man who would execute for him sketches and paintings of all that in the districts passed through was worthy of record. He had already 'heard Kniep highly spoken of as a clever draughtsman—only his industry was not much commended.' Our hearts sink. 'I have tolerably studied his character, and think the ground of this censure arises rather from a want of decision, which may certainly be overcome, if we are long together.' Our hearts sink lower. Kniep will never do. Kniep will play the deuce, we are sure of it. And yet (such is life) Kniep turns out very well. Throughout the Sicilian tour Goethe gives the rosiest reports of the young man's cheerful ways and strict attention to the business of sketching. It may be that these reports were coloured partly by a desire to set Tischbein down. But there seems to be no doubt that Goethe liked Kniep greatly and rejoiced in the quantity and quality of his work. At Palermo, one evening, Goethe sat reading Homer and 'making an impromptu translation for the benefit of Kniep, who had well deserved by his diligent exertions this day some agreeable refreshment over a glass of wine.' This is a pleasing little scene, and is typical of the whole tour.

In the middle of May, Goethe returned Naples. And lo!—Tischbein was not there to receive him. Tischbein, if you please, had skipped back to Rome, bidding his Neapolitan friends look to his great compatriot. Pride again forbade Goethe to show displeasure, and again our reading has to be done between the lines. In the first week of June he was once more in Rome. I can imagine with what high courtesy, as though there were nothing to rebuke, he treated Tischbein. But it is possible that his manner would have been less perfect had the portrait not been unfinished.

His sittings were resumed. It seems that Signora Zucchi, better known to the world as Angelica Kauffmann, had also begun to paint him. But, great as was Goethe's esteem for the mind of that nice woman, he set no store on this fluttering attempt of hers: 'her picture is a pretty fellow, to be sure, but not a trace of me.' It was by the large and firm 'historic' mode of Tischbein that he, not exactly in his habit as he lived, but in the white mantle that so well became him, and on the worthy throne of that fallen obelisk, was to be handed down to the gaze of future ages. Was to be, yes. On June 27th he reports that Tischbein's work 'is succeeding happily; the likeness is striking, and the conception pleases everybody.' Three days later: 'Tischbein goes to Naples.'

Incredible! We stare aghast, as in the presence of some great dignitary from behind whom, by a ribald hand, a chair is withdrawn when he is in the act of sitting down. Tischbein had, as it were, withdrawn the obelisk. What was Goethe to do? What can a dignitary, in such case, do? He cannot turn and recriminate. That would but lower him the more. Can he behave as though nothing has happened? Johann Wolfgang von Goethe tried to do so. And it must have been in support of this attempt that he consented to leave his own quarters and reside awhile in the studio of the outgoing Tischbein. That slippery man does, it is true, seem to have given out that he would not be away very long; and the prospect of his return may well have been reckoned in mitigation of his going. Goethe had leave from the Duke of Weimar to prolong his Italian holiday till the spring of next year. It is possible that Tischbein really did mean to come back and finish the picture. Goethe had, at any rate, no reason for not hoping.

'When you think of me, think of me as happy,' he directs. And had he not indeed reasons for happiness? He had the most perfect health, he was writing masterpieces, he was in Rome—Rome which no pilgrim had loved with a rapture deeper than his; the wonderful old Rome that lingered on almost to our own day, under the conserving shadow of the Temporal Power; a Rome in which the Emperors kept unquestionably their fallen day about them. No pilgrim had wandered with a richer enthusiasm along those highways and those great storied spaces. It is pleasing to watch in what deep draughts Goethe drank Rome in. But—but—I fancy that now in his second year of sojourn he tended to remain within the city walls, caring less than of yore for the Campagna; and I suspect that if ever he did stray out there he averted his eyes from anything in the nature of a ruined temple. Of one thing I am sure. The huge canvas in the studio had its face to the wall. There is never a reference to it by Goethe in any letter after that of June 27th. But I surmise that its nearness continually worked on him, and that sometimes, when no one was by, he all unwillingly approached it, he moved it out into a good light and, stepping back, gazed at it for a long time. And I wonder that Tischbein was not shamed, telepathically, to return.

What was it that had made Tischbein—not once, but thrice—abandon Goethe? We have no right to suppose he had plotted to avenge himself for the poet's refusal to collaborate with him on the theme of primaeval man. A likelier explanation is merely that Goethe, as I have suggested, irked him. Forty years elapsed before Goethe collected his letters from Italy and made a book of them; and in this book he included—how magnanimous old men are!—several letters written to him from Naples by his deserter. These are shallow but vivid documents—the effusions of one for whom the visible world suffices. I take it that Tischbein was an 'historic' painter because no ambitious painter in those days wasn't. In Goethe the historic sense was as innate as the aesthetic; so was the ethical sense; so was the scientific sense; and the three of them, forever cropping up in his discourse, may well be understood to have been too much for the simple Tischbein. But, you ask, can mere boredom make a man act so cruelly as this man acted? Well, there may have been another cause, and a more interesting one. I have mentioned that Goethe and Tischbein visited our Ambassador in Naples. His Excellency was at that time a widower, but his establishment was already graced by his future wife, Miss Emma Harte, whose beauty is so well known to us all. 'Tischbein,' wrote Goethe a few days afterwards, 'is engaged in painting her.' Later in the year, Tischbein, soon after his return to Naples, sent to Goethe a sketch for a painting he had now done of Miss Harte as Iphigenia at the Sacrificial Altar. Perhaps he had wondered that she should sacrifice herself to Sir William Hamilton.... 'I like Hamilton uncommonly' is a phrase culled from one of his letters; and when a man is very hearty about the protector of a very beautiful woman one begins to be suspicious. I do not mean to suggest that Miss Harte—though it is true she had not yet met Nelson—was fascinated by Tischbein. But we have no reason to suppose that Tischbein was less susceptible than Romney.

Altogether, it seems likely enough that the future Lady Hamilton's fine eyes were Tischbein's main reason for not going to Sicily, and afterwards for his sudden exodus from Rome. But why, in this case, did he leave Naples, why go back to Rome, when Goethe was in Sicily? I hope he went for the purpose of shaking off his infatuation for Miss Harte. I am loth to think he went merely to wind up his affairs in Rome. I will assume that only after a sharp conflict, in which he fought hard on the side of duty against love, did he relapse to Naples. But I won't pretend to wish he had finished that portrait.

If you know where that portrait is, tell me. I want it. I have tried to trace it—vainly. What became of it? I thought I might find this out in George Henry Lewes' 'Life of Goethe.' But Lewes had a hero-worship for Goethe: he thought him greater than George Eliot, and in the whole book there is but one cold mention of Tischbein's name. Mr. Oscar Browning, in the 'Encyclopaedia Britannica,' names Tischbein as Goethe's 'constant companion' in the early days at Rome—and says nothing else about him! In fact, the hero-worshippers have evidently conspired to hush up the affront to their hero. Even the 'Penny Cyclopaedia' (1842), which devotes a column to little Tischbein himself, and goes into various details of his career, is silent about the portrait of Goethe. I learn from that column that Tischbein became director of the Neapolitan Academy, at a salary of 600 ducats, and resided in Naples until the Revolution of '99, when he returned in haste to Germany. Suppose he passed through Rome on his way. A homing fugitive would not pause to burden himself with a vast unfinished canvas. We may be sure the canvas remained in that Roman studio—an object of mild interest to successive occupants. Is it there still? Does the studio itself still exist? Belike it has been demolished, with so much else. What became of the expropriated canvas? It wouldn't have been buried in the new foundations. Some one must have staggered away with it. Whither? Somewhere, I am sure, in some dark vault or cellar, it languishes.

Seek it, fetch it out, bring it to me in triumph. You will always find me in the Baptistery of San Lorenzo. But I have formed so clear and sharp a preconception of the portrait that I am likely to be disappointed at sight of what you bring me. I see in my mind's eye every falling fold of the white mantle; the nobly-rounded calf of the leg on which rests the forearm; the high-light on the black silk stocking. The shoes, the hands, are rather sketchy, the sky is a mere slab; the ruined temples are no more than adumbrated. But the expression of the face is perfectly, epitomically, that of a great man surveying a great alien scene and gauging its import not without a keen sense of its dramatic conjunction with himself—Marius in Carthage and Napoleon before the Sphinx, Wordsworth on London Bridge and Cortes on the peak in Darien, but most of all, certainly, Goethe in the Campagna. So, you see, I cannot promise not to be horribly let down by Tischbein's actual handiwork. I may even have to take back my promise that it shall have a place of honour. But I shall not utterly reject it—unless on the plea that a collection of unfinished works should itself have some great touch of incompletion.

SOMETHING DEFEASIBLE

July, 1919

The cottage had a good trim garden in front of it, and another behind it. I might not have noticed it at all but for them and their emerald greenness. Yet itself (I saw when I studied it) was worthy of them. Sussex is rich in fine Jacobean cottages; and their example, clearly, had not been lost on the builder of this one. Its proportions had a homely grandeur. It was long and wide and low. It was quite a yard long. It had three admirable gables. It had a substantial and shapely chimney-stack. I liked the look that it had of honest solidity all over, nothing anywhere scamped in the workmanship of it. It looked as though it had been built for all time. But this was not so. For it was built on sand, and of sand; and the tide was coming in.

Here and there in its vicinity stood other buildings. None of these possessed any points of interest. They were just old-fashioned 'castles,' of the bald and hasty kind which I myself used to make in childhood and could make even now—conic affairs, with or without untidily-dug moats, the nullities of convention and of unskilled labour. When I was a child the charm of a castle was not in the building of it, but in jumping over it when it was built. Nor was this an enduring charm. After a few jumps one abandoned one's castle and asked one's nurse for a bun, or picked a quarrel with some child even smaller than oneself, or went paddling. As it was, so it is. My survey of the sands this morning showed me that forty years had made no difference. Here was plenty of animation, plenty of scurrying and gambolling, of laughter and tears. But the actual spadework was a mere empty form. For all but the builder of that cottage. For him, manifestly, a passion, a rite.

He stood, spade in hand, contemplating, from one angle and another, what he had done. He was perhaps nine years old; if so, small for his age. He had very thin legs in very short grey knickerbockers, a pale freckled face, and hair that matched the sand. He was not remarkable. But with a little good-will one can always find something impressive in anybody. When Mr. Mallaby-Deeley won a wide and very sudden fame in connexion with Covent Garden, an awe-stricken reporter wrote of him for The Daily Mail, 'he has the eyes of a dreamer.' I believe that Mr. Cecil Rhodes really had. So, it seemed to me, had this little boy. They were pale grey eyes, rather prominent, with an unwavering light in them. I guessed that they were regarding the cottage rather as what it should be than as what it had become. To me it appeared quite perfect. But I surmised that to him, artist that he was, it seemed a poor thing beside his first flushed conception.

He knelt down and, partly with the flat of his spade, partly with the palm of one hand, redressed some (to me obscure) fault in one of the gables. He rose, stood back, his eyes slowly endorsed the amendment. A few moments later, very suddenly, he scudded away to the adjacent breakwater and gave himself to the task of scraping off it some of the short green sea-weed wherewith he had made the cottage's two gardens so pleasantly realistic, oases so refreshing in the sandy desert. Were the lawns somehow imperfect? Anon, when he darted back, I saw what it was that his taste had required: lichen, moss, for the roof. Sundry morsels and patches of green he deftly disposed in the angles of roof and gables. His stock exhausted, off to the breakwater he darted, and back again, to and fro with the lightning directness of a hermit-bee making its nest of pollen. The low walls that enclosed the two gardens were in need of creepers. Little by little, this grace was added to them. I stood silently watching.

I kept silent for fear of discommoding him. All artists—by which I mean, of course, all good artists—are shy. They are trustees of something not entrusted to us others; they bear fragile treasure, not safe in a jostling crowd; they must ever be wary. And especially shy are those artists whose work is apart from words. A man of letters can mitigate his embarrassment among us by a certain glibness. Not so can the man who works through the medium of visual form and colour. Not so, I was sure, could the young architect and landscape-gardener here creating. I would have moved away had I thought my mere presence was a bother to him; but I decided that it was not: being a grown-up person, I did not matter; he had no fear that I should offer violence to his work. It was his coevals that made him uneasy. Groups of these would pause in their wild career to stand over him and watch him in a fidgety manner that hinted mischief. Suppose one of them suddenly jumped—on to the cottage!

Fragile treasure, this, in a quite literal sense; and how awfully exposed! It was spared, however. There was even legible on the faces of the stolid little boys who viewed it a sort of reluctant approval. Some of the little girls seemed to be forming with their lips the word 'pretty,' but then they exchanged glances with one another, signifying 'silly.' No one of either sex uttered any word of praise. And so, because artists, be they never so agoraphobious, do want praise, I did at length break my silence to this one. 'I think it splendid,' I said to him.

He looked up at me, and down at the cottage. 'Do you?' he asked, looking up again. I assured him that I did; and to test my opinion of him I asked whether he didn't think so too. He stood the test well. 'I wanted it rather diff'rent,' he answered.

'In what way different?'

He searched his vocabulary. 'More comf'table,' he found.

I knew now that he was not merely the architect and builder of the cottage, but also, by courtesy of imagination, its tenant;

but I was tactful enough not to let him see that I had guessed this deep and delicate secret. I did but ask him, in a quite general way, how the cottage could be better. He said that it ought to have a porch—'but porches tumble in.' He was too young an artist to accept quite meekly the limits imposed by his material. He pointed along the lower edge of the roof: 'It ought to stick out,' he said, meaning that it wanted eaves. I told him not to worry about that: it was the sand's fault, not his. 'What really is a pity,' I said, 'is that your house can't last for ever.' He was tracing now on the roof, with the edge of his spade, a criss-cross pattern, to represent tiles, and he seemed to have forgotten my presence and my kindness. 'Aren't you sorry,' I asked, raising my voice rather sharply, 'that the sea is coming in?'

He glanced at the sea. 'Yes.' He said this with a lack of emphasis that seemed to me noble though insincere.

The strain of talking in words of not more than three syllables had begun to tell on me. I bade the artist good-bye, wandered away up the half-dozen steps to the Parade, sat down on a bench, and opened the morning paper that I had brought out unread. During the War one felt it a duty to know the worst before breakfast; now that the English polity is threatened merely from within, one is apt to dally.... Merely from within? Is that a right phrase when the nerves of unrestful Labour in any one land are interplicated with its nerves in any other, so vibrantly? News of the dismissal of an erring workman in Timbuctoo is enough nowadays to make us apprehensive of vast and dreadful effects on our own immediate future. How pleasant if we had lived our lives in the nineteenth century and no other, with the ground all firm under our feet! True, the people who flourished then had recurring alarms. But their alarms were quite needless; whereas ours—! Ours, as I glanced at this morning's news from Timbuctoo and elsewhere, seemed odiously needful. Withal, our Old Nobility in its pleasaunces was treading once more the old graceful measure which the War arrested; Bohemia had resumed its motley; even the middle class was capering, very noticeably... To gad about smiling as though he were quite well, thank you, or to sit down, pull a long face, and make his soul,—which, I wondered, is the better procedure for a man knowing that very soon he will have to undergo a vital operation at the hands of a wholly unqualified surgeon who dislikes him personally? I inclined to think the gloomier way the less ghastly. But then, I asked myself, was my analogy a sound one? We are at the mercy of Labour, certainly; and Labour does not love us; and Labour is not deeply versed in statecraft. But would an unskilled surgeon, however ill-wishing, care to perform a drastic operation on a patient by whose death he himself would forthwith perish? Labour is wise enough—surely?—not to will us destruction. Russia has been an awful example. Surely! And yet, Labour does not seem to think the example so awful as I do. Queer, this; queer and disquieting. I rose from my bench, strolled to the railing, and gazed forth.

The unrestful, the well-organised and minatory sea had been advancing quickly. It was not very far now from the cottage. I thought of all the civilisations that had been, that were not, that were as though they had never been. Must it always be thus?—always the same old tale of growth and greatness and overthrow, nothingness? I gazed at the cottage, all so solid and seemly, so full of endearing character, so like to the 'comf'table' polity of England as we have known it. I gazed away from it to a large-ish castle that the sea was just reaching. A little, then quickly much, the waters swirled into the moat. Many children stood by, all a-dance with excitement. The castle was shedding its sides, lapsing, dwindling, land-slipping—gone. O Nineveh! And now another—O Memphis? Rome?—yielded to the cataclysm. I listened to the jubilant screams of the children. What rapture, what wantoning! Motionless beside his work stood the builder of the cottage, gazing seaward, a pathetic little figure. I hoped the other children would have the decency not to exult over the unmaking of what he had made so well. This hope was not fulfilled. I had not supposed it would be. What did surprise me, when anon the sea rolled close up to the cottage, was the comportment of the young artist himself. His sobriety gave place to an intense animation. He leapt, he waved his spade, he invited the waves with wild gestures and gleeful cries. His face had flushed bright, and now, as the garden walls crumbled, and the paths and lawns were mingled by the waters' influence and confluence, and the walls of the cottage itself began to totter, and the gables sank, and all, all was swallowed, his leaps were so high in air that they recalled to my memory those of a strange religious sect which once visited London; and the glare of his eyes was less indicative of a dreamer than of a triumphant fiend.

I myself was conscious of a certain wild enthusiasm within me. But this was less surprising for that I had not built the cottage, and my fancy had not enabled me to dwell in it. It was the boy's own enthusiasm that made me feel, as never before, how deep-rooted in the human breast the love of destruction, of mere destruction, is. And I began to ask myself: 'Even if England as we know it, the English polity of which that cottage was a symbol to me, were the work of (say) Mr. Robert Smillie's own unaided hands'—but I waived the question coming from that hypothesis, and other questions that would have followed; for I wished to be happy while I might.

'A CLERGYMAN'

1918

Fragmentary, pale, momentary; almost nothing; glimpsed and gone; as it were, a faint human hand thrust up, never to reappear, from beneath the rolling waters of Time, he forever haunts my memory and solicits my weak imagination. Nothing is told of him but that once, abruptly, he asked a question, and received an answer.

This was on the afternoon of April 7th, 1778, at Streatham, in the well-appointed house of Mr. Thrale. Johnson, on the morning of that day, had entertained Boswell at breakfast in Bolt Court, and invited him to dine at Thrale Hall. The two took coach and arrived early. It seems that Sir John Pringle had asked Boswell to ask Johnson 'what were the best English sermons for style.' In the interval before dinner, accordingly, Boswell reeled off the names of several divines whose prose might or might not win commendation. 'Atterbury?' he suggested. 'JOHNSON: Yes, Sir, one of the best. BOSWELL: Tillotson? JOHNSON: Why, not now. I should not advise any one to imitate Tillotson's style; though I don't know; I should be cautious of censuring anything that has been applauded by so many suffrages.—South is one of the best, if you except his peculiarities, and his violence, and sometimes coarseness of language.—Seed has a very fine style; but he is not very theological. Jortin's sermons are very elegant. Sherlock's style, too, is very elegant, though he has not made it his principal study.—And you may add Smalridge.

BOSWELL: I like Ogden's Sermons on Prayer very much, both for neatness of style and subtilty of reasoning. JOHNSON: I should like to read all that Ogden has written. BOSWELL: What I want to know is, what sermons afford the best specimen of English pulpit eloquence. JOHNSON: We have no sermons addressed to the passions, that are good for anything; if you mean that kind of eloquence. A CLERGYMAN, whose name I do not recollect: Were not Dodd's sermons addressed to the passions? JOHNSON: They were nothing, Sir, be they addressed to what they may.'

The suddenness of it! Bang!—and the rabbit that had popped from its burrow was no more.

I know not which is the more startling—the de'but of the unfortunate clergyman, or the instantaneousness of his end. Why hadn't Boswell told us there was a clergyman present? Well, we may be sure that so careful and acute an artist had some good reason. And I suppose the clergyman was left to take us unawares because just so did he take the company. Had we been told he was there, we might have expected that sooner or later he would join in the conversation. He would have had a place in our minds. We may assume that in the minds of the company around Johnson he had no place. He sat forgotten, overlooked; so that his self-assertion startled every one just as on Boswell's page it startles us. In Johnson's massive and magnetic presence only some very remarkable man, such as Mr. Burke, was sharply distinguishable from the rest. Others might, if they had something in them, stand out slightly. This unfortunate clergyman may have had something in him, but I judge that he lacked the gift of seeming as if he had. That deficiency, however, does not account for the horrid fate that befell him. One of Johnson's strongest and most inveterate feelings was his veneration for the Cloth. To any one in Holy Orders he habitually listened with a grave and charming deference. To-day moreover, he was in excellent good humour. He was at the Thrales', where he so loved to be; the day was fine; a fine dinner was in close prospect; and he had had what he always declared to be the sum of human felicity—a ride in a coach. Nor was there in the question put by the clergyman anything likely to enrage him. Dodd was one whom Johnson had befriended in adversity; and it had always been agreed that Dodd in his pulpit was very emotional. What drew the blasting flash must have been not the question itself, but the manner in which it was asked. And I think we can guess what that manner was.

Say the words aloud: 'Were not Dodd's sermons addressed to the passions?' They are words which, if you have any dramatic and histrionic sense, cannot be said except in a high, thin voice.

You may, from sheer perversity, utter them in a rich and sonorous baritone or bass. But if you do so, they sound utterly unnatural. To make them carry the conviction of human utterance, you have no choice: you must pipe them.

Remember, now, Johnson was very deaf. Even the people whom he knew well, the people to whose voices he was accustomed, had to address him very loudly. It is probable that this unregarded, young, shy clergyman, when at length he suddenly mustered courage to 'cut in,' let his high, thin voice soar too high, insomuch that it was a kind of scream. On no other hypothesis can we account for the ferocity with which Johnson turned and rended him. Johnson didn't, we may be sure, mean to be cruel. The old lion, startled, just struck out blindly. But the force of paw and claws was not the less lethal. We have endless testimony to the strength of Johnson's voice; and the very cadence of those words, 'They were nothing, Sir, be they addressed to what they may,' convinces me that the old lion's jaws never gave forth a louder roar. Boswell does not record that there was any further conversation before the announcement of dinner. Perhaps the whole company had been temporarily deafened. But I am not bothering about them. My heart goes out to the poor dear clergyman exclusively.

I said a moment ago that he was young and shy; and I admit

that I slipped those epithets in without having justified them to you by due process of induction. Your quick mind will have already supplied what I omitted. A man with a high, thin voice, and without power to impress any one with a sense of his importance, a man so null in effect that even the retentive mind of Boswell did not retain his very name, would assuredly not be a self-confident man. Even if he were not naturally shy, social courage would soon have been sapped in him, and would in time have been destroyed, by experience. That he had not yet given himself up as a bad job, that he still had faint wild hopes, is proved by the fact that he did snatch the opportunity for asking that question. He must, accordingly, have been young. Was he the curate of the neighbouring church? I think so. It would account for his having been invited. I see him as he sits there listening to the great Doctor's pronouncement on Atterbury and those others. He sits on the edge of a chair in the background. He has colourless eyes, fixed earnestly, and a face almost as pale as the clerical bands beneath his somewhat receding chin. His forehead is high and narrow, his hair mouse-coloured. His hands are clasped tight before him, the knuckles standing out sharply. This constriction does not mean that he is steeling himself to speak. He has no positive intention of speaking. Very much, nevertheless, is he wishing in the back of his mind that he could say something—something whereat the great Doctor would turn on him and say, after a pause for thought, 'Why yes, Sir. That is most justly observed' or 'Sir, this has never occurred to me. I thank you'-thereby fixing the observer for ever high in the esteem of all. And now in a flash the chance presents itself. 'We have,' shouts Johnson, 'no sermons addressed to the passions, that are good for anything.' I see the curate's frame quiver with sudden impulse, and his mouth fly open, and—no, I can't bear it, I shut my eyes and ears. But audible, even so, is something shrill, followed by something thunderous.

Presently I re-open my eyes. The crimson has not yet faded from that young face yonder, and slowly down either cheek falls a glistening tear. Shades of Atterbury and Tillotson! Such weakness shames the Established Church. What would Jortin and Smalridge have said?—what Seed and South? And, by the way, who were they, these worthies? It is a solemn thought that so little is conveyed to us by names which to the palaeo-Georgians conveyed so much. We discern a dim, composite picture of a big man in a big wig and a billowing black gown, with a big congregation beneath him. But we are not anxious to hear what he is saying. We know it is all very elegant. We know it will be printed and be bound in finely-tooled full calf, and no palaeo-Georgian gentleman's library will be complete without it. Literate people in those days were comparatively few; but, bating that, one may say that sermons were as much in request as novels are to-day. I wonder, will mankind continue to be capricious? It is a very solemn thought indeed that no more than a hundred-and-fifty years hence the novelists of our time, with all their moral and political and sociological outlook and influence, will perhaps shine as indistinctly as do those old preachers, with all their elegance, now. 'Yes, Sir,' some great pundit may be telling a disciple at this moment, 'Wells is one of the best. Galsworthy is one of the best, if you except his concern for delicacy of style. Mrs. Ward has a very firm grasp of problems, but is not very creational.—Caine's books are very edifying. I should like to read all that Caine has written. Miss Corelli, too, is very edifying.—And you may add Upton Sinclair.' 'What I want to know,' says the disciple, 'is, what English novels may be selected as specially enthralling.' The pundit answers: 'We have no novels addressed to the passions that are good for anything, if you mean that kind of enthralment.' And here some poor wretch (whose name the disciple will not remember) inquires: 'Are not Mrs. Glyn's novels addressed to the passions?' and is in due form annihilated. Can it be that a time will come when readers of this passage in our pundit's Life will take more interest in the poor nameless wretch than in all the bearers of those great names put together, being no more able or anxious to discriminate between (say) Mrs. Ward and Mr. Sinclair than we are to set Ogden above Sherlock, or Sherlock above Ogden? It seems impossible. But we must remember that things are not always what they seem.

Every man illustrious in his day, however much he may be gratified by his fame, looks with an eager eye to posterity for a continuance of past favours, and would even live the remainder of his life in obscurity if by so doing he could insure that future generations would preserve a correct attitude towards him forever. This is very natural and human, but, like so many very natural and human things, very silly. Tillotson and the rest need not, after all, be pitied for our neglect of them. They either know nothing about it, or are above such terrene trifles. Let us keep our pity for the seething mass of divines who were not elegantly verbose, and had no fun or glory while they lasted. And let us keep a specially large portion for one whose lot was so much worse than merely undistinguished. If that nameless curate had not been at the Thrales' that day, or, being there, had kept the silence that so well became him, his life would have been drab enough, in all conscience. But at any rate an unpromising career would not have been nipped in the bud. And that is what in fact happened, I'm sure of it. A robust man might have rallied under the blow. Not so our friend. Those who knew him in infancy had not expected that he would be reared. Better for him had they been right. It is well to grow up and be ordained, but not if you are delicate and very sensitive, and shall happen to annoy the greatest, the most stentorian and roughest of contemporary personages. 'A Clergyman' never held up his head or smiled again after the brief encounter recorded for us by Boswell. He sank into a rapid decline. Before the next blossoming of Thrale Hall's almond trees he was no more. I like to think that he died forgiving Dr. Johnson.

THE CRIME

1920

On a bleak wet stormy afternoon at the outset of last year's Spring, I was in a cottage, all alone, and knowing that I must be all alone till evening. It was a remote cottage, in a remote county, and had been 'let furnished' by its owner. My spirits are easily affected by weather, and I hate solitude. And I dislike to be master of things that are not mine. 'Be careful not to break us,' say the glass and china. 'You'd better not spill ink on me,' growls the carpet. 'None of your dog's-earing, thumb-marking, back-breaking tricks here!' snarl the books.

The books in this cottage looked particularly disagreeable—horrid little upstarts of this and that scarlet or cerulean 'series' of 'standard' authors. Having gloomily surveyed them, I turned my back on them, and watched the rain streaming down the latticed window, whose panes seemed likely to be shattered at any moment by the wind. I have known men who constantly visit the Central Criminal Court, visit also the scenes where famous crimes were committed, form their own theories of those crimes, collect souvenirs of those crimes, and call themselves Criminologists. As for me, my interest in crime is, alas, merely morbid. I did not know, as those others would doubtless have known, that the situation in which I found myself was precisely of the kind most conducive to the darkest deeds. I did but bemoan it, and think of Lear in the hovel on the heath. The wind howled in the chimney, and the rain had begun to sputter right down it, so that the fire was beginning to hiss in a very sinister manner. Suppose the fire went out! It looked as if it meant to. I snatched the pair of bellows that hung beside it. I plied them vigorously. 'Now mind!—not too vigorously. We aren't yours!' they wheezed. I handled them more gently. But I did not release them till they had secured me a steady blaze.

I sat down before that blaze. Despair had been warded off. Gloom, however, remained; and gloom grew. I felt that I should prefer any one's thoughts to mine. I rose, I returned to the books. A dozen or so of those which were on the lowest of the three shelves were full-sized, were octavo, looked as though they had been bought to be read. I would exercise my undoubted right to read one of them. Which of them? I gradually decided on a novel by a well-known writer whose works, though I had several times had the honour of meeting her, were known to me only by repute.

I knew nothing of them that was not good. The lady's 'output' had not been at all huge, and it was agreed that her 'level' was high. I had always gathered that the chief characteristic of her work was its great 'vitality.' The book in my hand was a third edition of her latest novel, and at the end of it were numerous press-notices, at which I glanced for confirmation. 'Immense vitality,' yes, said one critic. 'Full,' said another, 'of an intense vitality.' 'A book that will live,' said a third. How on earth did he know that? I was, however, very willing to believe in the vitality of this writer for all present purposes. Vitality was a thing in which she herself, her talk, her glance, her gestures, abounded. She and they had been, I remembered, rather too much for me. The first time I met her, she said something that I lightly and mildly disputed. On no future occasion did I stem any opinion of hers. Not that she had been rude. Far from it. She had but in a sisterly, brotherly way, and yet in a way that was filially eager too, asked me to explain my point. I did my best. She was all attention. But I was conscious that my best, under her eye, was not good. She was quick to help me: she said for me just what I had tried to say, and proceeded to show me just why it was wrong. I smiled the gallant smile of a man who regards women as all the more adorable because logic is not their strong point, bless them! She asked—not aggressively, but strenuously, as one who dearly loves a joke—what I was smiling at. Altogether, a chastening encounter; and my memory of it was tinged with a feeble resentment. How she had scored! No man likes to be worsted in argument by a woman. And I fancy that to be vanquished by a feminine writer is the kind of defeat least of all agreeable to a man who writes. A 'sex war,' we are often told is to be one of the features of the world's future—women demanding the right to do men's work, and men refusing, resisting, counter-attacking. It seems likely enough. One can believe anything of the world's future. Yet one conceives that not all men, if this particular evil come to pass, will stand packed shoulder to shoulder against all women. One does not feel that the dockers will be very bitter against such women as want to be miners, or the plumbers frown much upon the would-be steeple-jills. I myself have never had my sense of fitness jarred, nor a spark of animosity roused in me, by a woman practising any of the fine arts—except the art of writing. That she should write a few little poems or pense'es, or some impressions of a trip in a dahabieh as far as (say) Biskra, or even a short story or two, seems to me not wholly amiss, even though she do such things for publication. But that she should be an habitual, professional author, with a passion for her art, and a fountain-pen and an agent, and sums down in advance of royalties on sales in Canada and Australia, and a profound knowledge of human character, and an essentially sane outlook, is somehow incongruous with my notions—my mistaken notions, if you will—of what she ought to be.

'Has a profound knowledge of human character, and an essentially sane outlook' said one of the critics quoted at the end of the book that I had chosen. The wind and the rain in the chimney had not abated, but the fire was bearing up bravely. So would I. I would read cheerfully and without prejudice. I poked the fire and, pushing my chair slightly back, lest the heat should warp the book's covers, began Chapter I. A woman sat writing in a summer-house at the end of a small garden that overlooked a great valley in Surrey. The description of her was calculated to make her very admirable—a thorough woman, not strictly beautiful, but likely to be thought beautiful by those who knew her well; not dressed as though she gave much heed to her clothes, but dressed in a fashion that exactly harmonised with her special type. Her pen 'travelled' rapidly across the foolscap, and while it did so she was described in more and more detail. But at length she came to a 'knotty point' in what she was writing. She paused, she pushed back the hair from her temples, she looked forth at the valley; and now the landscape was described, but not at all exhaustively, it, for the writer soon overcame her difficulty, and her pen travelled faster than ever, till suddenly there was a cry of 'Mammy!' and in rushed a seven-year-old child, in conjunction with whom she was more than ever admirable; after which the narrative skipped back across eight years, and the woman became a girl, giving as yet no token of future eminence in literature but—I had an impulse which I obeyed almost before I was, conscious of it.

Nobody could have been more surprised than I was at what I had done—done so neatly, so quietly and gently. The book stood closed, upright, with its back to me, just as on a bookshelf, behind the bars of the grate. There it was. And it gave forth, as the flames crept up the blue cloth sides of it, a pleasant though acrid smell. My astonishment had passed, giving place to an exquisite satisfaction. How pottering and fumbling a thing was even the best kind of written criticism! I understood the contempt felt by the man of action for the man of words. But what pleased me most was that at last, actually, I, at my age, I of all people, had committed a crime—was guilty of a crime. I had power to revoke it. I might write to my bookseller for an unburnt copy, and place it on the shelf where this one had stood—this gloriously glowing one. I would do nothing of the sort. What I had done I had done. I would wear forever on my conscience the white rose of theft and the red rose of arson. If hereafter the owner of this cottage happened to miss that volume—let him! If he were fool enough to write to me about it, would I share my grand secret with him? No.

Gently, with his poker, I prodded that volume further among the coals. The all-but-consumed binding shot forth little tongues of bright colour—flamelets of sapphire, amethyst, emerald. Charming! Could even the author herself not admire them? Perhaps. Poor woman!—I had scored now, scored so perfectly that I felt myself to be almost a brute while I poked off the loosened black outer pages and led the fire on to pages that were but pale brown.

These were quickly devoured. But it seemed to me that whenever I left the fire to forage for itself it made little headway. I pushed the book over on its side. The flames closed on it, but presently, licking their lips, fell back, as though they had had enough. I took the tongs and put the book upright again, and raked it fore and aft. It seemed almost as thick as ever. With poker and tongs I carved it into two, three sections—the inner pages flashing white as when they were sent to the binders. Strange! Aforetime, a book was burnt now and again in the market-place by the common hangman. Was he, I wondered, paid by the hour? I had always supposed the thing quite easy for him—a bright little, brisk little conflagration, and so home. Perhaps other books were less resistant than this one? I began to feel that the critics were more right than they knew. Here was a book that had indeed an intense vitality, and an immense vitality. It was a book that would live—do what one might. I vowed it should not. I subdivided it, spread it, redistributed it. Ever and anon my eye would be caught by some sentence or fragment of a sentence in the midst of a charred page before the flames crept over it. 'lways loathed you, bu', I remember; and 'ning. Tolstoi was right.' Who had always loathed whom? And what, what, had Tolstoi been right about? I had an absurd but genuine desire to know. Too late! Confound the woman!—she was scoring again. I furiously drove her pages into the yawning crimson jaws of the coals. Those jaws had lately been golden. Soon, to my horror, they seemed to be growing grey. They seemed to be closing—on nothing. Flakes of black paper, full-sized layers of paper brown and white, began to hide them from me altogether. I sprinkled a boxful of wax matches. I resumed the bellows. I lunged with the poker. I held a newspaper over the whole grate. I did all that inspiration could suggest, or skill accomplish. Vainly. The fire went out—darkly, dismally, gradually, quite out.

How she had scored again! But she did not know it. I felt no bitterness against her as I lay back in my chair, inert, listening to the storm that was still raging. I blamed only myself. I had done wrong. The small room became very cold. Whose fault was that but my own? I had done wrong hastily, but had done it and been glad of it. I had not remembered the words a wise king wrote long ago, that the lamp of the wicked shall be put out, and that the way of trangressors is hard.

IN HOMES UNBLEST

1919

Nothing is more pleasant than to see suddenly endowed with motion a thing stagnant by nature. The hat that on the head of the man in the street is nothing to us, how much it is if it be animated by a gust of wind! There is no churl that does not rejoice with it in its strength, and in the swiftness and cunning that baffle its pursuer, who, he too, when the chase is over, bears it no ill will at all for its escapade. I know families that have sat for hours, for hours after bedtime, mute, in a dim light, pressing a table with their finger-tips, and ever bringing to bear the full force of their minds on it, in the unconquerable hope that it would move. Conversely, nothing is more dismal than to see set in permanent rigidity a thing whose aspect is linked for us with the idea of great mobility. Even the blithest of us and least easily depressed would make a long detour to avoid a stuffed squirrel or a case of pinned butterflies. And you can well imagine with what a sinking of the heart I beheld, this morning, on a road near the coast of Norfolk, a railway-car without wheels.

Without wheels though it was, it had motion—of a kind; of a kind worse than actual stagnation. Mounted on a very long steam-lorry that groaned and panted, it very slowly passed me. I noted that two of its compartments were marked FIRST, the rest THIRD. And in some of them, I noted, you might smoke. But of this opportunity you were not availing yourself. All the compartments, the cheap and the dear alike, were vacant. They were transporting air only—and this (I conceived) abominable. The sun slanted fiercely down on the old iron roof, the old wooden walls, the dingy shut windows. The fume and grime of a thousand familiar tunnels, of year after year of journeys by night, journeys by day, from time immemorial, seemed to have invested the whole structure with a character that shrank from the sun's scrutiny and from the nearness of sea and fields. Fuliginous, monstrous, slowly, shamefully, the thing went by—to what final goal?—in the lovely weather.

There attended it, besides the driver of the lorry, a straggling retinue of half-a-dozen men on foot—handy-looking mechanics, very dusty. I should have liked to question one or another of these as to their mission. But I was afraid to do so. There is an art of talking acceptably to people who do not regard themselves as members of one's own class; and I have never acquired it. I suppose the first step is to forget that any art is needed-to forget that one must not be so wildly cordial for fear of seeming to 'condescend,' nor be more than a trifle saturnine, either, for the same motive. Or am I wrong? The whole thing is a mystery to me. All I know is that if I had asked those mechanics what they were doing with that railway car they would have seemed to suspect me of meaning that it was my property and that they had stolen it. Or perhaps they would have seemed merely to resent my idle curiosity. If so, why not? When I walk abroad with a sheaf of manuscript in my hand, mechanics do not stop me to ask 'What's that? What's it about? Who's going to publish it?' Nor is this because, times having changed so, they are afraid of seeming to condescend. They always did mind their own business. And now that their own business is so much more lucrative than mine they still follow that golden rule.

I stood gazing back at the procession till it disappeared round a bend of the road. Its bequest of dust and smoke was quickly spent by a prodigal young breeze. Landscape and seascape were reindued with their full amenities. Ruskin would have been pleased. So indeed was I; but that railway-car (in which, it romantically struck me, I myself might once, might frequently, have travelled) was still upmost in my brooding mind. To what manner of wretched end was it destined? No end would have seemed bad enough for it to Ruskin. But I was born late enough to acquiesce in railways and in all that pertains to them. And now, since the success of motor-cars (those far greater, because unrestricted, bores), railways have taken on for me some such charm as the memory of the posting coaches had for the greybeards of my boyhood, some such charm as aeroplanes may in the fulness of time foist down for us on motor-cars. 'But I rove,' like Sir Thomas More. And I seem to think that a cheap literary allusion will make you excuse that vice. To resume my breathless narrative I decided that I would slowly follow the tracks of the lorry.

I supposed that these were leading me to some great scrapping-place filled with the remains of other railway-cars foully scrapped for some fell industrial purpose. But this was a bad guess. The tracks led me at last through a lane and thence into sight of a little bay, on whose waters were perceptible the deck heads of sundry human beings, and on its sands the full-lengths of sundry other human beings in bath-robes, reading novels or merely basking. There was nowhere any sign of industrialism. More than ever was I intrigued as to the fate of the old railway-car that I had been stalking. It and its lorry had halted on the flat grassy land that fringed the sands. This land was dominated by a crescent of queer little garish tenements, the like of which I had never seen, nor would wish to see again. They did not stand on the ground, but on stakes of wood and shafts of brick, six feet or so above the ground's level, and were led up to by flights of wooden steps that tried not to look like ladders. They displeased me much. They had little railed platforms round them, and things hanging out to dry on the railings; and their walls vied unneighbourly with one another in lawless colour-schemes. One tenement was salmon-pink with wide bands of scarlet, another sky-blue with a key-pattern in orange, and so on around the whole little horrid array. And I deduced, from certain upstanding stakes and shafts at the nearer end of the crescent, that the horror was not complete yet. A suspicion dawned in me, and became, while I gazed again at the crescent's facades, a glaring certainty; in the light of which I saw that I had been wrong about the old railway-car. Defunct, it was not to die. It was to have a new function.

I had once heard that disused railway-cars were convertible into sea-side cottages. But the news had not fired my imagination nor protruded in my memory. To-day, as an eye-witness of the accomplished fact, I was impressed, sharply enough, and I went nearer to the crescent, drawn by a sort of dreadful fascination. I found that the cottages all had names. One cottage was Mermaid's Rock; another (which had fluttering window-curtains of Stuart tartan), Spray o' the Sea; another, The Nest; another, Brinynook; and yet another had been named, with less fitness, but in an ampler and to me more interesting spirit, Petworth. I looked from them to the not-yet-converted railway-car. It had a wonderful dignity. In its austere and monumental way, it was very beautiful. It was a noble work of man, and Nature smiled on it. I wondered with what colours it was to be bejezebelled, and what name—Bolton Abbey?—Glad Eye?—Gay Wee Gehenna?—it would have to bear, and what manner of man or woman was going to rent it.

It was on this last point that I mused especially. The housing problem is hard, doubtless; but nobody, my mind protested as I surveyed the crescent, nobody is driven to so desperate a solution of it as this! There are tents, there are caves, there are hollow trees...and there are people who prefer—this! Yes, 'this' is a positive taste, not a necessity at all. I swept the bay with a searching eye; but heads on the surface of water tell nothing to the sociologist, and in bath-robes even full-lengths on the sand give him no clue. Three or four of the full-lengths had risen and strolled up to the lorry, around which the mechanics were engaged in some dispute of a technical nature. I hoped the full-lengths would have something to say too. But they said nothing. This I set down to sheer perversity. I was more than three miles from the place where I am sojourning, and the hour for luncheon was nearly due. I left the bay without having been able to determine the character, the kind, of its denizens.

I take it there is a strong tincture of Bohemianism in them. Mr. Desmond MacCarthy, of whose judgment I am always trustful, has said that the hallmark of Bohemianism is a tendency to use things for purposes to which they are not adapted. You are a Bohemian, says Mr. MacCarthy, if you would gladly use a razor for buttering your toast at breakfast, and you aren't if you wouldn't. I think he would agree that the choice of a home is a surer index than any fleeting action, however strange, and that really the best-certified Bohemians are they who choose to reside in railway-cars on stilts. But— why particularly railway-cars? That is a difficult question. A possible answer is that the Bohemian, as tending always to nomady, feels that the least uncongenial way of settling down is to stow himself into a thing fashioned for darting hither and thither. Yet no, this answer won't do. It is ruled out by the law I laid down in my first paragraph. There's nothing sadder to eye or heart than a very mobile thing made immovable.

No house, especially if you are by way of being nomadic, can be so ill to live in as one that in its heyday went gadding all over the place. And, on the other hand, what house more eligible than one that can gad? I myself am not restless, and am fond of comfort: I should not care to live in a caravan. But I have always liked the idea of a caravan. And if you, alas, O reader, are a dweller in a railway-car, I commend the idea to you. Take it, with my apologies for any words of mine that may have nettled you. Put it into practice. Think of the white road and the shifting hedgerows, and the counties that you will soon lose count of. And think what a blessing it will be for you to know that your house is not the one in which the Merstham Tunnel murder was committed.

WILLIAM AND MARY

1920

Memories, like olives, are an acquired taste. William and Mary (I give them the Christian names that were indeed theirs—the joint title by which their friends always referred to them) were for some years an interest in my life, and had a hold on my affection. But a time came when, though I had known and liked them too well ever to forget them, I gave them but a few thoughts now and then. How, being dead, could they keep their place in the mind of a young man surrounded with large and constantly renewed consignments of the living? As one grows older, the charm of novelty wears off. One finds that there is no such thing as novelty—or, at any rate, that one has lost the faculty for perceiving it. One sees every newcomer not as something strange and special, but as a ticketed specimen of this or that very familiar genus. The world has ceased to be remarkable; and one tends to think more and more often of the days when it was so very remarkable indeed.

I suppose that had I been thirty years older when first I knew him, William would have seemed to me little worthier of attention than a twopenny postage-stamp seems to-day. Yet, no: William really had some oddities that would have caught even an oldster's eye. In himself he was commonplace enough (as I, coeval though I was with him, soon saw). But in details of surface he was unusual. In them he happened to be rather ahead of his time. He was a socialist, for example. In 1890 there was only one other socialist in Oxford, and he not at all an undergraduate, but a retired chimney-sweep, named Hines, who made speeches, to which nobody, except perhaps William, listened, near the Martyrs' Memorial. And William wore a flannel shirt, and rode a bicycle—very strange habits in those days, and very horrible. He was said to be (though he was short-sighted and wore glasses) a first-rate 'back' at football; but, as football was a thing frowned on by the rowing men, and coldly ignored by the bloods, his talent for it did not help him: he was one of the principal pariahs of our College; and it was rather in a spirit of bravado, and to show how sure of myself I was, that I began, in my second year, to cultivate his acquaintance.

We had little in common. I could not think Political Economy 'the most exciting thing in the world,' as he used to call it. Nor could I without yawning listen to more than a few lines of Mr. William Morris' interminable smooth Icelandic Sagas, which my friend, pious young socialist that he was, thought 'glorious.' He had begun to write an Icelandic Saga himself, and had already achieved some hundreds of verses. None of these pleased him, though to me they seemed very like his master's. I can see him now, standing on his hearth-rug, holding his MS. close to his short-sighted eyes, declaiming the verses and trying, with many angular gestures of his left hand, to animate them—a tall, broad, raw-boned fellow, with long brown hair flung back from his forehead, and a very shabby suit of clothes. Because of his clothes and his socialism, and his habit of offering beer to a guest, I had at first supposed him quite poor; and I was surprised when he told me that he had from his guardian (his parents being dead) an allowance of œ350, and that when he came of age he would have an income of œ400. 'All out of dividends,' he would groan. I would hint that Mr. Hines and similar zealots might disembarrass him of this load, if he asked them nicely. 'No,' he would say quite seriously, 'I can't do that,' and would read out passages from 'Fabian Essays' to show that in the present anarchical conditions only mischief could result from sporadic dispersal of rent. 'Ten, twelve years hence—' he would muse more hopefully. 'But by that time,' I would say, 'you'll probably be married, and your wife mightn't quite—', whereat he would hotly repeat what he had said many times: that he would never marry. Marriage was an anti-social anachronism. I think its survival was in some part due to the machinations of Capital. Anyway, it was doomed. Temporary civil contracts between men and women would be the rule 'ten, twelve years hence'; pending which time the lot of any man who had civic sense must be celibacy, tempered perhaps with free love.

Long before that time was up, nevertheless, William married. One afternoon in the spring of '95 I happened to meet him at a corner of Cockspur Street. I wondered at the immense cordiality of his greeting; for our friendship, such as it was, had waned in our two final years at Oxford. 'You look very flourishing, and,' I said, 'you're wearing a new suit!' 'I'm married,' he replied, obviously without a twinge of conscience. He told me he had been married just a month. He declared that to be married was the most splendid thing in all the world; but he weakened the force of this generalisation by adding that there never was any one like his wife. 'You must see her,' he said; and his impatience to show her proudly off to some one was so evident, and so touching, that I could but accept his invitation to go and stay with them for two or three days—'why not next week?' They had taken and furnished 'a sort of cottage' in —shire, and this was their home. He had 'run up for the day, on business—journalism' and was now on his way to Charing Cross. 'I know you'll like my wife,' he said at parting. She's—well, she's glorious.'

As this was the epithet he had erst applied to 'Beowulf' and to 'Sigurd the Volsung' it raised no high hopes. And indeed, as I was soon to find, he had again misused it. There was nothing glorious about his bride. Some people might even have not thought her pretty. I myself did not, in the flash of first sight. Neat, insignificant, pleasing, was what she appeared to me, rather than pretty, and far rather than glorious. In an age of fringes, her brow was severely bare. She looked 'practical.' But an instant later, when she smiled, I saw that she was pretty, too. And presently I thought her delightful. William had met me in a 'governess cart,' and we went to see him unharness the pony. He did this in a fumbling, experimental way, confusing the reins with the traces, and profiting so little by his wife's directions that she began to laugh. And her laugh was a lovely thing; quite a small sound, but exquisitely clear and gay, coming in a sequence of notes that neither rose nor fell, that were quite even; a trill of notes, and then another, and another, as though she were pulling repeatedly a little silver bell... As I describe it, perhaps the sound may be imagined irritating. I can only say it was enchanting.

I wished she would go on laughing; but she ceased, she darted forward and (William standing obediently aside, and I helping unhelpfully) unharnessed the pony herself, and led it into its small stable. Decidedly, she was 'practical,' but—I was prepared now to be lenient to any quality she might have.

Had she been feckless, no doubt I should have forgiven her that, too; but I might have enjoyed my visit less than I did, and might have been less pleased to go often again. I had expected to 'rough it' under William's roof. But everything thereunder, within the limits of a strict Arcadian simplicity, was well-ordered. I was touched, when I went to my bedroom, by the precision with which the very small maid had unpacked and disposed my things. And I wondered where my hostess had got the lore she had so evidently imparted. Certainly not from William. Perhaps (it only now strikes me) from a handbook. For Mary was great at handbooks. She had handbooks about gardening, and others about poultry, and one about 'the stable,' and others on cognate themes. From these she had filled up the gaps left in her education by her father, who was a widower and either a doctor or a solicitor—I forget which—in one of the smallest towns of an adjoining county. And I daresay she may have had, somewhere hidden away, a manual for young hostesses. If so, it must have been a good one. But to say this is to belittle Mary's powers of intuition. It was they, sharpened by her adoration of William, and by her intensity for everything around him, that made her so efficient a housewife.

If she possessed a manual for young house-hunters it was assuredly not by the light of this that she had chosen the home they were installed in. The 'sort of cottage' had been vacant for many years—an unpromising and ineligible object, a mile away from a village, and three miles away from a railway station. The main part of it was an actual cottage, of seventeenth-century workmanship; but a little stuccoed wing had been added to each side of it, in 1850 or thereabouts, by an eccentric old gentleman who at that time chose to make it his home. He had added also the small stable, a dairy, and other appanages. For these, and for garden, there was plenty of room, as he had purchased and enclosed half an acre of the surrounding land Those two stuccoed, very Victorian wings of his, each with a sash-window above and a French window below, consorted queerly with the old red brick and the latticed panes. And the long wooden veranda that he had invoked did not unify the trinity. But one didn't want it to. The wrongness had a character all its own. The wrongness was right—at any rate after Mary had hit on it for William. As a spinster, she would, I think, have been happiest in a trim modern villa. But it was a belief of hers that she had married a man of strange genius. She had married him for himself, not for his genius; but this added grace in him was a thing to be reckoned with, ever so much; a thing she must coddle to the utmost in a proper setting. She was a year older than he (though, being so small and slight, she looked several years younger), and in her devotion the maternal instinct played a great part. William, as I have already conveyed to you, was not greatly gifted. Mary's instinct, in this one matter, was at fault. But endearingly, rightly at fault. And, as William was outwardly odd, wasn't it well that his home should be so, too? On the inside, comfort was what Mary always aimed at for him, and achieved.

The ground floor had all been made one room, into which you stepped straight from the open air. Quite a long big room (or so it seemed, from the lowness of the ceiling), and well-freshened in its antiquity, with rush-mats here and there on the irregular red tiles, and very white whitewash on the plaster between the rafters. This was the dining-room, drawing-room, and general focus throughout the day, and was called simply the Room. William had a 'den' on the ground floor of the left wing; and there, in the mornings, he used to write a great deal. Mary had no special place of her own: her place was wherever her duties needed her. William wrote reviews of books for the Daily —. He did also creative work. The vein of poetry in him had worked itself out—or rather, it expressed itself for him in Mary. For technical purposes, the influence of Ibsen had superseded that of Morris. At the time of my first visit, he was writing an extraordinarily gloomy play about an extraordinarily unhappy marriage. In subsequent seasons (Ibsen's disc having been somehow eclipsed for him by George Gissing's) he was usually writing novels in which every one—or do I exaggerate?—had made a disastrous match. I think Mary's belief in his genius had made him less diffident than he was at Oxford. He was always emerging from his den, with fresh pages of MS., into the Room. 'You don't mind?' he would say, waving his pages, and then would shout 'Mary!' She was always promptly forthcoming—sometimes from the direction of the kitchen, in a white apron, sometimes from the garden, in a blue one. She never looked at him while he read. To do so would have been lacking in respect for his work. It was on this that she must concentrate her whole mind, privileged auditor that she was. She sat looking straight before her, with her lips slightly compressed, and her hands folded on her lap. I used to wonder that there had been that first moment when I did not think her pretty. Her eyes were of a very light hazel, seeming all the lighter because her hair was of so dark a brown; and they were beautifully set in a face of that 'pinched oval' kind which is rather rare in England. Mary as listener would have atoned to me for any defects there may have been in dear old William's work. Nevertheless, I sometimes wished this work had some comic relief in it. Publishers, I believe, shared this wish; hence the eternal absence of William's name from among their announcements. For Mary's sake, and his, I should have liked him to be 'successful.' But at any rate he didn't need money. He didn't need, in addition to what he had, what he made by his journalism. And as for success—well, didn't Mary think him a genius? And wasn't he Mary's husband? The main reason why I wished for light passages in what he read to us was that they would have been cues for Mary's laugh. This was a thing always new to me. I never tired of that little bell-like euphony; those funny little lucid and level trills.

There was no stint of that charm when William was not reading to us. Mary was in no awe of him, apart from his work, and in no awe at all of me: she used to laugh at us both, for one thing and another—just the same laugh as I had first heard when William tried to unharness the pony. I cultivated in myself whatever amused her in me; I drew out whatever amused her in William; I never let slip any of the things that amused her in herself. 'Chaff' is a great bond; and I should have enjoyed our bouts of it even without Mary's own special obbligato. She used to call me (for I was very urban in those days) the Gentleman from London. I used to call her the Brave Little Woman. Whatever either of us said or did could be twisted easily into relation to those two titles; and our bouts, to which William listened with a puzzled, benevolent smile, used to cease only because Mary regarded me as a possible purveyor of what William, she was sure, wanted and needed, down there in the country, alone with her: intellectual conversation, after his work. She often, I think, invented duties in garden or kitchen so that he should have this stimulus, or luxury, without hindrance. But when William was alone with me it was about her that he liked to talk, and that I myself liked to talk too. He was very sound on the subject of Mary; and so was I. And if, when I was alone with Mary, I seemed to be sounder than I was on the subject of William's wonderfulness, who shall blame me?

Had Mary been a mother, William's wonderfulness would have been less greatly important. But he was her child as well as her lover. And I think, though I do not know, she believed herself content that this should always be, if so it were destined. It was not destined so. On the first night of a visit I paid them in April, 1899, William, when we were alone, told me news. I had been vaguely conscious, throughout the evening, of some change; conscious that Mary had grown gayer, and less gay—somehow different, somehow remote. William said that her child would be born in September, if all went well. 'She's immensely happy,' he told me. I realised that she was indeed happier than ever... 'And of course it would be a wonderful thing, for both of us,' he said presently, 'to have a son—or a daughter.' I asked him which he would rather it were, a son or a daughter. 'Oh, either,' he answered wearily. It was evident that he had misgivings and fears. I tried to reason him out of them. He did not, I am thankful to say, ever let Mary suspect them. She had no misgivings. But it was destined that her child should live only for an hour, and that she should die in bearing it.

I had stayed again at the cottage in July, for some days. At the end of that month I had gone to France, as was my custom, and a week later had written to Mary. It was William that answered this letter, telling me of Mary's death and burial. I returned to England next day. William and I wrote to each other several times. He had not left his home. He stayed there, 'trying,' as he said in a grotesque and heart-rending phrase, 'to finish a novel.' I saw him in the following January. He wrote to me from the Charing Cross Hotel, asking me to lunch with him there. After our first greetings, there was a silence. He wanted to talk of—what he could not talk of. We stared helplessly at each other, and then, in the English way, talked of things at large. England was engaged in the Boer War. William was the sort of man whom one would have expected to be violently Pro-Boer. I was surprised at his fervour for the stronger side. He told me he had tried to enlist, but had been rejected on account of his eyesight. But there was, he said, a good chance of his being sent out, almost immediately, as one of the Daily —'s special correspondents. 'And then,' he exclaimed, 'I shall see something of it.' I had a presentiment that he would not return, and a belief that he did not want to return. He did not return. Special correspondents were not so carefully shepherded in that war as they have since been. They were more at liberty to take risks, on behalf of the journals to which they were accredited. William was killed a few weeks after he had landed at Cape Town.

And there came, as I have said, a time when I did not think of William and Mary often; and then a time when I did more often think of them. And especially much did my mind hark back to them in the late autumn of last year; for on the way to the place I was staying at I had passed the little railway station whose name had always linked itself for me with the names of those two friends. There were but four intervening stations. It was not a difficult pilgrimage that I made some days later— back towards the past, for that past's sake and honour. I had thought I should not remember the way, the three miles of way, from the station to the cottage; but I found myself remembering it perfectly, without a glance at the finger-posts. Rain had been falling heavily, driving the late leaves off the trees; and everything looked rather sodden and misty, though the sun was now shining. I had known this landscape only in spring, summer, early autumn. Mary had held to a theory that at other seasons I could not be acclimatised. But there were groups of trees that I knew, even without their leaves; and farm-houses and small stone bridges that had not at all changed. Only what mattered was changed. Only what mattered was gone. Would what I had come to see be there still? In comparison with what it had held, it was not much. But I wished to see it, melancholy spectacle though it must be for me if it were extant, and worse than melancholy if it held something new. I began to be sure it had been demolished, built over. At the corner of the lane that had led to it, I was almost minded to explore no further, to turn back. But I went on, and suddenly I was at the four-barred iron gate, that I remembered, between the laurels. It was rusty, and was fastened with a rusty padlock, and beyond it there was grass where a winding 'drive' had been. From the lane the cottage never had been visible, even when these laurels were lower and sparser than they were now. Was the cottage still standing? Presently, I climbed over the gate, and walked through the long grass, and—yes, there was Mary's cottage; still there; William's and Mary's cottage. Trite enough, I have no doubt, were the thoughts that possessed me as I stood gazing. There is nothing new to be thought about the evanescence of human things; but there is always much to be felt about it by one who encounters in his maturity some such intimate instance and reminder as confronted me, in that cold sunshine, across that small wilderness of long rank wet grass and weeds.

Incredibly woebegone and lonesome the house would have looked even to one for whom it contained no memories; all the more because in its utter dereliction it looked so durable. Some of the stucco had fallen off the walls of the two wings; thick flakes of it lay on the discoloured roof of the veranda, and thick flakes of it could be seen lying in the grass below. Otherwise, there were few signs of actual decay. The sash-window and the French window of each wing were shuttered, and, from where I was standing, the cream-coloured paint of those shutters behind the glass looked almost fresh. The latticed windows between had all been boarded up from within. The house was not to be let perish soon.

I did not want to go nearer to it; yet I did go nearer, step by step, across the wilderness, right up to the edge of the veranda itself, and within a yard of the front-door.

I stood looking at that door. I had never noticed it in the old days, for then it had always stood open. But it asserted itself now, master of the threshold.

It was a narrow door—narrow even for its height, which did not exceed mine by more than two inches or so; a door that even when it was freshly painted must have looked mean. How much meaner now, with its paint all faded and mottled, cracked and blistered! It had no knocker, not even a slit for letters. All that it had was a large-ish key-hole. On this my eyes rested; and presently I moved to it, stooped down to it, peered through it. I had a glimpse of—darkness impenetrable.

Strange it seemed to me, as I stood back, that there the Room was, the remembered Room itself, separated from me by nothing but this unremembered door...and a quarter of a century, yes. I saw it all, in my mind's eye, just as it had been: the way the sunlight came into it through this same doorway and through the lattices of these same four windows; the way the little bit of a staircase came down into it, so crookedly yet so confidently; and how uneven the tiled floor was, and how low the rafters were, and how littered the whole place was with books brought in from his den by William, and how bright with flowers brought in by Mary from her garden. The rafters, the stairs, the tiles, were still existing, changeless in despite of cobwebs and dust and darkness, all quite changeless on the other side of the door, so near to me. I wondered how I should feel if by some enchantment the door slowly turned on its hinges, letting in light. I should not enter, I felt, not even look, so much must I hate to see those inner things lasting when all that had given to them a meaning was gone from them, taken away from them, finally. And yet, why blame them for their survival? And how know that nothing of the past ever came to them, revisiting, hovering? Something—sometimes—perhaps? One knew so little. How not be tender to what, as it seemed to me, perhaps the dead loved?

So strong in me now was the wish to see again all those things, to touch them and, as it were, commune with them, and so queerly may the mind be wrought upon in a solitude among memories, that there were moments when I almost expected that the door would obey my will. I was recalled to a clearer sense of reality by something which I had not before noticed. In the door-post to the right was a small knob of rusty iron—mocking reminder that to gain admission to a house one does not 'will' the door: one rings the bell—unless it is rusty and has quite obviously no one to answer it; in which case one goes away. Yet I did not go away. The movement that I made, in despite of myself, was towards the knob itself. But, I hesitated, suppose I did what I half meant to do, and there were no sound. That would be ghastly. And surely there would be no sound. And if sound there were, wouldn't that be worse still? My hand drew back, wavered, suddenly closed on the knob. I heard the scrape of the wire—and then, from somewhere within the heart of the shut house, a tinkle.

It had been the weakest, the puniest of noises. It had been no more than is a fledgling's first attempt at a twitter. But I was not judging it by its volume. Deafening peals from steeples had meant less to me than that one single note breaking the silence—in there. In there, in the dark, the bell that had answered me was still quivering, I supposed, on its wire. But there was no one to answer it, no footstep to come hither from those recesses, making prints in the dust. Well, I could answer it; and again my hand closed on the knob, unhesitatingly this time, pulling further. That was my answer; and the rejoinder to it was more than I had thought to hear—a whole quick sequence of notes, faint but clear, playful, yet poignantly sad, like a trill of laughter echoing out of the past, or even merely out of this neighbouring darkness. It was so like something I had known, so recognisable and, oh, recognising, that I was lost in wonder. And long must I have remained standing at that door, for I heard the sound often, often. I must have rung again and again, tenaciously, vehemently, in my folly.

ON SPEAKING FRENCH

1919

Wherever two Englishmen are speaking French to a Frenchman you may safely diagnose in the breast of one of the two humiliation, envy, ill-will, impotent rage, and a dull yearning for vengeance; and you can take it that the degree of these emotions is in exact ratio to the superiority of the other man's performance. In the breast of this other are contempt, malicious amusement, conceit, vanity, pity, and joy in ostentation; these, also, exactly commensurable with his advantage. Strange and sad that this should be so; but so it is. French brings out the worst in all of us—all, I mean, but the few, the lamentably far too few, who cannot aspire to stammer some colloquial phrases of it.

Even in Victorian days, when England was more than geographically, was psychologically an island, French made mischief among us, and was one of the Devil's favourite ways of setting brother against brother. But in those days the bitterness of the weaker brother was a little sweetened with disapproval of the stronger. To speak French fluently and idiomatically and with a good accent—or with an idiom and accent which to other rough islanders seemed good—was a rather suspect accomplishment, being somehow deemed incompatible with civic worth. Thus the weaker ones had not to drain the last lees of their shame, and the stronger could not wholly rejoice in their strength. But the old saving prejudice has now died out (greatly to the delight of the Devil), and there seems no chance that it will be revived.

Of other languages no harm comes. None of us—none, at any rate, outside the diplomatic service—has a feeling that he ought to be master of them. In every recent generation a few men have learned Italian because of the Divina Commedia; and a very few others have tried Spanish, with a view to Cervantes; and German has pestered not always vainly the consciences of young men gravitating to philosophy or to science. But not for social, not for any oral purposes were these languages essayed. If an Italian or a Spanish or a German came among us he was expected to converse in English or spend his time in visiting the sights silently and alone. No language except French has ever—but stay! There was, at the outbreak of the War, a great impulse towards Russian. All sorts of people wanted their children to be taught Russian without a moment's delay. I do not remember that they wanted to learn it themselves; but they felt an extreme need that their offspring should hereafter be able to converse with moujiks about ikons and the Little Father and anything else—if there were anything else—that moujiks cared about. This need, however, is not felt now. When, so soon after his de'but in high politics, M. Kerensky was superseded by M. Lenin, Russian was forthwith deemed a not quite nice language, even for children. Russia's alphabet was withdrawn from the nurseries as abruptly as it had been brought in, and le chapean de la cousine du jardinier was re-indued with its old importance.

I doubt whether Russian would for more than a little while have seemed to be a likely rival of French, even if M. Kerensky had been the strong man we hoped he was. The language that succeeded to Latin as the official mode of intercourse between nations, and as the usual means of talk between the well-educated people of any one land and those of any other, had an initial advantage not quite counterbalanced by the fact that there are in Russia myriads of people who speak Russian, and a few who can also read and write it. Russian may, for aught I know, be a very beautiful language; it may be as lucid and firm in its constructions as French is, and as musical in sound; I know nothing at all about it. Nor do I claim for French that it was by its own virtues predestined to the primacy that it holds in Europe. Had Italy, not France, been an united and powerful nation when Latin became desuete, that primacy would of course have been taken by Italian. And I cannot help wishing that this had happened. Italian, though less elegant, is, for the purpose of writing, a richer language than French, and an even subtler; and the sound of it spoken is as superior to the sound of French as a violin's is to a flute's. Still, French does, by reason of its exquisite concision and clarity, fill its post of honour very worthily, and will not in any near future, I think, be thrust down. Many people, having regard to the very numerous population of the British Empire and the United States, cherish a belief that English will presently be cock of the world's walk. But we have to consider that English is an immensely odd and irregular language, that it is accounted very difficult by even the best foreign linguists, and that even among native writers there are few who can so wield it as to make their meaning clear without prolixity—and among these few none who has not been well-grounded in Latin. By its very looseness, by its way of evoking rather than defining, suggesting rather than saying, English is a magnificent vehicle for emotional poetry. But foreigners don't much want to say beautiful haunting things to us; they want to be told what limits there are, if any, to the power of the Lord Mayor; and our rambling endeavours to explain do but bemuse and annoy them. They find that the rewards of learning English are as slight as its difficulties are great, and they warn their fellows to this effect. Nor does the oral sound of English allay the prejudice thus created. Soothing and dear and charming that sound is to English ears. But no nation can judge the sound of its own language. This can be judged only from without, only by ears to which it is unfamiliar. And alas, much as we like listening to French or Italian, for example, Italians and Frenchmen (if we insist on having their opinion) will confess that English has for them a rather harsh sound. Altogether, it seems to me unlikely that the world will let English supplant French for international purposes, and likely that French will be ousted only when the world shall have been so internationalised that the children of every land will have to learn, besides their own traditional language, some kind of horrible universal lingo begotten on Volapuk by a congress of the world's worst pedants.

Almost I could wish I had been postponed to that era, so much have I suffered through speaking French to Frenchmen in the presence of Englishmen. Left alone with a Frenchman, I can stumble along, slowly indeed, but still along, and without acute sense of ignominy. Especially is this so if I am in France. There is in the atmosphere something that braces one for the language. I don't say I am not sorry, even so, for my Frenchman. But I am sorrier for him in England. And if any Englishmen be included in the scene my sympathy with him is like to be lost in my agony for myself.

Would that I had made some such confession years ago! O folly of pride! I liked the delusion that I spoke French well, a delusion common enough among those who had never heard me. Somehow I seemed likely to possess that accomplishment. I cannot charge myself with having ever claimed to possess it; but I am afraid that when any one said to me 'I suppose you speak French perfectly?' I allowed the tone of my denial to carry with it a hint of mock-modesty. 'Oh no,' I would say, 'my French is wretched,' rather as though I meant that a member of the French Academy would detect lapses from pure classicism in it; or 'No, no, mine is French pour rire,' to imply that I was practically bilingual. Thus, during the years when I lived in London, I very often received letters from hostesses asking me to dine on the night when Mme. Chose or M. Tel was coming. And always I excused myself—not on the plea that I should be useless. This method of mine would have been well enough, from any but the moral standpoint, had not Nemesis, taking her stand on that point, sometimes ordained that a Gaul should be sprung on me. It was not well with me then. It was downfall and disaster.

Strange, how one will trifle with even the most imminent doom. On being presented to the Gaul, I always hastened to say that I spoke his or her language only 'un tout petit peu'—knowing well that this poor spark of slang would kindle within the breast of M. Tel or the bosom of Mme. Chose hopes that must so quickly be quenched in the puddle of my incompetence. I offer no excuse for so foolish a proceeding. I do but say it is characteristic of all who are duffers at speaking a foreign tongue. Great is the pride they all take in airing some little bit of idiom. I recall, among many other pathetic exemplifiers of the foible, an elderly and rather eminent Greek, who, when I was introduced to him, said 'I am jolly glad to meet you, Sir!' and, having said that, had nothing whatever else to say, and was moreover unable to grasp the meaning of anything said by me, though I said the simplest things, and said them very slowly and clearly. It is to my credit that in speaking English to a foreigner I do always try to be helpful. I bear witness against Mme. Chose and M. Tel that for me they have never made a like effort in their French. It is said that French people do not really speak faster than we, and that their seeming to do so is merely because of their lighter stress on syllables. If this is true, I wish that for my sake they would stress their syllables a little more heavily. By their omission of this kindness I am so often baffled as to their meaning. To be shamed as a talker is bad enough; it is even worse to be shamed in the humble refuge of listener. To listen and from time to time murmur 'C'est vrai' may seem safe enough; yet there is danger even here. I wish I could forget a certain luncheon in the course of which Mme. Chose (that brilliant woman) leaned suddenly across the table to me, and, with great animation, amidst a general hush, launched at me a particularly swift flight of winged words. With pensively narrowed eyes, I uttered my formula when she ceased. This formula she repeated, in a tone even more pensive than mine. 'Mais je ne le connais pas,' she then loudly exclaimed. 'Je ne connais pas me^me le nom. Dites-moi de ce jeune homme.' She had, as it presently turned out, been asking me which of the younger French novelists was most highly thought of by English critics; so that her surprise at never having heard of the gifted young Se'vre' was natural enough.

We all—but no, I must not say that we all have painful memories of this kind. Some of us can understand every word that flies from the lips of Mme. Chose or from the mouth of M. Tel. Some of us can also talk quickly and well to either of these pilgrims; and others can do the trick passably. But the duffers are in a great grim majority; and the mischief that French causes among us is mainly manifest, not (I would say) by weaker brethren hating the stronger, but by weak ones hating the less weak.

As French is a subject on which we all feel so keenly, a point of honour on which we are all so sensitive, how comes it that our general achievement is so slight? There was no lack of hopes, of plans, that we should excel. In many cases Time was taken for us by the forelock, and a French nurse installed. But alas! little children are wax to receive and to retain. They will be charmingly fluent speakers of French within six weeks of Mariette's arrival, and will have forgotten every word of it within as brief an interval after her departure. Later, their minds become more retentive, though less absorbent; and then, by all means, let French be taught. Taught it is. At the school where I was reared there were four French masters; four; but to what purpose? Their class-rooms were scenes of eternal and incredible pandemonium, filled with whoops and catcalls, with devil's-tattoos on desks, and shrill inquiries for the exact date of the battle of Waterloo. Nor was the lot of those four men exceptional in its horror. From the accounts given to me by 'old boys' of other schools I have gathered that it was the common lot of French masters on our shores; and I have often wondered how much of the Anglophobia recurrent among Frenchmen in the nineteenth century was due to the tragic tales told by those of them who had returned from our seminaries to die on their own soil. Since 1914, doubtless, French masters have had a very good time in England. But, even so, I doubt whether they have been achieving much in the way of tutelage. With the best will in the world, a boy will profit but little by three or four lessons a week (which are the utmost that our system allows him). What he wants, or at any rate will want, is to be able to cope with Mme. Chose. A smattering of the irregular verbs will not much avail him in that emprise. Not in the dark by-ways of conjugation, but on the sunny field of frank social intercourse, must he prove his knighthood. I would recommend that every boy, on reaching the age of sixteen, should be hurled across the Channel into the midst of some French family and kept there for six months. At the end of that time let him be returned to his school, there to make up for lost time. Time well lost, though: for the boy will have become fluent in French, and will ever remain so.

Fluency is all. If the boy has a good ear, he will speak with a good accent; but his accent is a point about which really he needn't care a jot. So is his syntax. Not with these will he win the heart of Mme. Chose, not with these the esteem of M. Tel, not with these anything but a more acrid rancour in the silly hostility of his competitors. If a foreigner speaks English to us easily and quickly, we demand no more of him; we are satisfied, we are delighted, and any mistakes of grammar or pronunciation do but increase the charm, investing with more than its intrinsic quality any good thing said—making us marvel at it and exchange fatuous glances over it, as we do when a little child says something sensible. But heaven protect us from the foreigner who pauses, searches, fumbles, revises, comes to standstills, has recourse to dumb-show! Away with him, by the first train to Dover! And this, we may be sure, is the very train M. Tel and Mme. Chose would like to catch whenever they meet me—or you?

LAUGHTER

1920

M. Bergson, in his well-known essay on this theme, says...well, he says many things; but none of these, though I have just read them, do I clearly remember, nor am I sure that in the act of reading I understood any of them. That is the worst of these fashionable philosophers—or rather, the worst of me. Somehow I never manage to read them till they are just going out of fashion, and even then I don't seem able to cope with them. About twelve years ago, when every one suddenly talked to me about Pragmatism and William James, I found myself moved by a dull but irresistible impulse to try Schopenhauer, of whom, years before that, I had heard that he was the easiest reading in the world, and the most exciting and amusing. I wrestled with Schopenhauer for a day or so, in vain. Time passed; M. Bergson appeared 'and for his hour was lord of the ascendant;' I tardily tackled William James. I bore in mind, as I approached him, the testimonials that had been lavished on him by all my friends. Alas, I was insensible to his thrillingness. His gaiety did not make me gay. His crystal clarity confused me dreadfully. I could make nothing of William James. And now, in the fullness of time, I have been floored by M. Bergson.

It distresses me, this failure to keep pace with the leaders of thought as they pass into oblivion. It makes me wonder whether I am, after all, an absolute fool. Yet surely I am not that. Tell me of a man or a woman, a place or an event, real or fictitious: surely you will find me a fairly intelligent listener. Any such narrative will present to me some image, and will stir me to not altogether fatuous thoughts. Come to me in some grievous difficulty: I will talk to you like a father, even like a lawyer. I'll be hanged if I haven't a certain mellow wisdom. But if you are by way of weaving theories as to the nature of things in general, and if you want to try those theories on some one who will luminously confirm them or powerfully rend them, I must, with a hang-dog air, warn you that I am not your man. I suffer from a strong suspicion that things in general cannot be accounted for through any formula or set of formulae, and that any one philosophy, howsoever new, is no better than another. That is in itself a sort of philosophy, and I suspect it accordingly; but it has for me the merit of being the only one I can make head or tail of. If you try to expound any other philosophic system to me, you will find not merely that I can detect no flaw in it (except the one great flaw just suggested), but also that I haven't, after a minute or two, the vaguest notion of what you are driving at. 'Very well,' you say, 'instead of trying to explain all things all at once, I will explain some little, simple, single thing.' It was for sake of such shorn lambs as myself, doubtless, that M. Bergson sat down and wrote about—Laughter. But I have profited by his kindness no more than if he had been treating of the Cosmos. I cannot tread even a limited space of air. I have a gross satisfaction in the crude fact of being on hard ground again, and I utter a coarse peal of—Laughter.

At least, I say I do so. In point of fact, I have merely smiled. Twenty years ago, ten years ago, I should have laughed, and have professed to you that I had merely smiled. A very young man is not content to be very young, nor even a young man to be young: he wants to share the dignity of his elders. There is no dignity in laughter, there is much of it in smiles. Laughter is but a joyous surrender, smiles give token of mature criticism. It may be that in the early ages of this world there was far more laughter than is to be heard now, and that aeons hence laughter will be obsolete, and smiles universal—every one, always, mildly, slightly, smiling. But it is less useful to speculate as to mankind's past and future than to observe men. And you will have observed with me in the club-room that young men at most times look solemn, whereas old men or men of middle age mostly smile; and also that those young men do often laugh loud and long among themselves, while we others—the gayest and best of us in the most favourable circumstances—seldom achieve more than our habitual act of smiling. Does the sound of that laughter jar on us? Do we liken it to the crackling of thorns under a pot? Let us do so. There is no cheerier sound. But let us not assume it to be the laughter of fools because we sit quiet. It is absurd to disapprove of what one envies, or to wish a good thing were no more because it has passed out of our possession.

But (it seems that I must begin every paragraph by questioning the sincerity of what I have just said) has the gift of laughter been withdrawn from me? I protest that I do still, at the age of forty-seven, laugh often and loud and long. But not, I believe, so long and loud and often as in my less smiling youth. And I am proud, nowadays, of laughing, and grateful to any one who makes me laugh. That is a bad sign. I no longer take laughter as a matter of course. I realise, even after reading M. Bergson on it, how good a thing it is. I am qualified to praise it.

As to what is most precious among the accessories to the world we live in, different men hold different opinions. There are people whom the sea depresses, whom mountains exhilarate. Personally, I want the sea always—some not populous edge of it for choice; and with it sunshine, and wine, and a little music. My friend on the mountain yonder is of tougher fibre and sterner outlook, disapproves of the sea's laxity and instability, has no ear for music and no palate for the grape, and regards the sun as a rather enervating institution, like central heating in a house. What he likes is a grey day and the wind in his face; crags at a great altitude; and a flask of whisky. Yet I think that even he, if we were trying to determine from what inner sources mankind derives the greatest pleasure in life, would agree with me that only the emotion of love takes higher rank than the emotion of laughter. Both these emotions are partly mental, partly physical. It is said that the mental symptoms of love are wholly physical in origin. They are not the less ethereal for that. The physical sensations of laughter, on the other hand, are reached by a process whose starting-point is in the mind. They are not the less 'gloriously of our clay.' There is laughter that goes so far as to lose all touch with its motive, and to exist only, grossly, in itself. This is laughter at its best. A man to whom such laughter has often been granted may happen to die in a work-house. No matter. I will not admit that he has failed in life. Another man, who has never laughed thus, may be buried in Westminster Abbey, leaving more than a million pounds overhead. What then? I regard him as a failure.

Nor does it seem to me to matter one jot how such laughter is achieved. Humour may rollick on high planes of fantasy or in depths of silliness. To many people it appeals only from those depths. If it appeal to them irresistibly, they are more enviable than those who are sensitive only to the finer kind of joke and not so sensitive as to be mastered and dissolved by it. Laughter is a thing to be rated according to its own intensity.

Many years ago I wrote an essay in which I poured scorn on the fun purveyed by the music halls, and on the great public for which that fun was quite good enough. I take that callow scorn back. I fancy that the fun itself was better than it seemed to me, and might not have displeased me if it had been wafted to me in private, in presence of a few friends. A public crowd, because of a lack of broad impersonal humanity in me, rather insulates than absorbs me. Amidst the guffaws of a thousand strangers I become unnaturally grave. If these people were the entertainment, and I the audience, I should be sympathetic enough. But to be one of them is a position that drives me spiritually aloof. Also, there is to me something rather dreary in the notion of going anywhere for the specific purpose of being amused. I prefer that laughter shall take me unawares. Only so can it master and dissolve me. And in this respect, at any rate, I am not peculiar. In music halls and such places, you may hear loud laughter, but—not see silent laughter, not see strong men weak, helpless, suffering, gradually convalescent, dangerously relapsing. Laughter at its greatest and best is not there.

To such laughter nothing is more propitious than an occasion that demands gravity. To have good reason for not laughing is one of the surest aids. Laughter rejoices in bonds. If music halls were schoolrooms for us, and the comedians were our schoolmasters, how much less talent would be needed for giving us how much more joy! Even in private and accidental intercourse, few are the men whose humour can reduce us, be we never so susceptible, to paroxysms of mirth. I will wager that nine tenths of the world's best laughter is laughter at, not with. And it is the people set in authority over us that touch most surely our sense of the ridiculous. Freedom is a good thing, but we lose through it golden moments. The schoolmaster to his pupils, the monarch to his courtiers, the editor to his staff—how priceless they are! Reverence is a good thing, and part of its value is that the more we revere a man, the more sharply are we struck by anything in him (and there is always much) that is incongruous with his greatness. And herein lies one of the reasons why as we grow older we laugh less. The men we esteemed so great are gathered to their fathers. Some of our coevals may, for aught we know, be very great, but good heavens! we can't esteem them so.

Of extreme laughter I know not in any annals a more satisfying example than one that is to be found in Moore's Life of Byron. Both Byron and Moore were already in high spirits when, on an evening in the spring of 1818, they went 'from some early assembly' to Mr. Rogers' house in St. James's Place and were regaled there with an impromptu meal. But not high spirits alone would have led the two young poets to such excess of laughter as made the evening so very memorable. Luckily they both venerated Rogers (strange as it may seem to us) as the greatest of living poets. Luckily, too, Mr. Rogers was ever the kind of man, the coldly and quietly suave kind of man, with whom you don't take liberties, if you can help it—with whom, if you can't help it, to take liberties is in itself a most exhilarating act. And he had just received a presentation copy of Lord Thurloe's latest book, 'Poems on Several Occasions.' The two young poets found in this elder's Muse much that was so execrable as to be delightful. They were soon, as they turned the pages, held in throes of laughter, laughter that was but intensified by the endeavours of their correct and nettled host to point out the genuine merits of his friend's work. And then suddenly—oh joy!— 'we lighted,' Moore records, 'on the discovery that our host, in addition to his sincere approbation of some of this book's contents, had also the motive of gratitude for standing by its author, as one of the poems was a warm and, I need not add, well-deserved panegyric on himself. We were, however'—the narrative has an added charm from Tom Moore's demure care not to offend or compromise the still-surviving Rogers—'too far gone in nonsense for even this eulogy, in which we both so heartily agreed, to stop us. The opening line of the poem was, as well as I can recollect, "When Rogers o'er this labour bent;" and Lord Byron undertook to read it aloud;—but he found it impossible to get beyond the first two words. Our laughter had now increased to such a pitch that nothing could restrain it. Two or three times he began; but no sooner had the words "When Rogers" passed his lips, than our fit burst out afresh,—till even Mr. Rogers himself, with all his feeling of our injustice, found it impossible not to join us; and we were, at last, all three in such a state of inextinguishable laughter, that, had the author himself been of our party, I question much whether he could have resisted the infection.' The final fall and dissolution of Rogers, Rogers behaving as badly as either of them, is all that was needed to give perfection to this heart-warming scene. I like to think that on a certain night in spring, year after year, three ghosts revisit that old room and (without, I hope, inconvenience to Lord Northcliffe, who may happen to be there) sit rocking and writhing in the grip of that old shared rapture. Uncanny? Well, not more so than would have seemed to Byron and Moore and Rogers the notion that more than a hundred years away from them was some one joining in their laughter—as I do.

Alas, I cannot join in it more than gently. To imagine a scene, however vividly, does not give us the sense of being, or even of having been, present at it. Indeed, the greater the glow of the scene reflected, the sharper is the pang of our realisation that we were not there, and of our annoyance that we weren't. Such a pang comes to me with special force whenever my fancy posts itself outside the Temple's gate in Fleet Street, and there, at a late hour of the night of May 10th, 1773, observes a gigantic old man laughing wildly, but having no one with him to share and aggrandise his emotion. Not that he is alone; but the young man beside him laughs only in politeness and is inwardly puzzled, even shocked. Boswell has a keen, an exquisitely keen, scent for comedy, for the fun that is latent in fine shades of character; but imaginative burlesque, anything that borders on lovely nonsense, he was not formed to savour. All the more does one revel in his account of what led up to the moment when Johnson 'to support himself, laid hold of one of the posts at the side of the foot pavement, and sent forth peals so loud that in the silence of the night his voice seemed to resound from Temple Bar to Fleet Ditch.'

No evening ever had an unlikelier ending. The omens were all for gloom. Johnson had gone to dine at General Paoli's, but was so ill that he had to leave before the meal was over. Later he managed to go to Mr. Chambers' rooms in the Temple. 'He continued to be very ill' there, but gradually felt better, and 'talked with a noble enthusiasm of keeping up the representation of respectable families,' and was great on 'the dignity and propriety of male succession.' Among his listeners, as it happened, was a gentleman for whom Mr. Chambers had that day drawn up a will devising his estate to his three sisters. The news of this might have been expected to make Johnson violent in wrath. But no, for some reason he grew violent only in laughter, and insisted thenceforth on calling that gentleman The Testator and chaffing him without mercy. 'I daresay he thinks he has done a mighty thing. He won't stay till he gets home to his seat in the country, to produce this wonderful deed: he'll call up the landlord of the first inn on the road; and after a suitable preface upon mortality and the uncertainty of life, will tell him that he should not delay in making his will;

and Here, Sir, will he say, is my will, which I have just made, with the assistance of one of the ablest lawyers in the kingdom; and he will read it to him. He believes he has made this will; but he did not make it; you, Chambers, made it for him. I hope you have had more conscience than to make him say "being of sound understanding!" ha, ha, ha! I hope he has left me a legacy. I'd have his will turned into verse, like a ballad.' These flights annoyed Mr. Chambers, and are recorded by Boswell with the apology that he wishes his readers to be 'acquainted with the slightest occasional characteristics of so eminent a man.' Certainly, there is nothing ridiculous in the fact of a man making a will. But this is the measure of Johnson's achievement. He had created gloriously much out of nothing at all. There he sat, old and ailing and unencouraged by the company, but soaring higher and higher in absurdity, more and more rejoicing, and still soaring and rejoicing after he had gone out into the night with Boswell, till at last in Fleet Street his paroxysms were too much for him and he could no more. Echoes of that huge laughter come ringing down the ages. But is there also perhaps a note of sadness for us in them? Johnson's endless sociability came of his inherent melancholy: he could not bear to be alone; and his very mirth was but a mode of escape from the dark thoughts within him. Of these the thought of death was the most dreadful to him, and the most insistent. He was for ever wondering how death would come to him, and how he would acquit himself in the extreme moment. A later but not less devoted Anglican, meditating on his own end, wrote in his diary that 'to die in church appears to be a great euthanasia, but not,' he quaintly and touchingly added, 'at a time to disturb worshippers.' Both the sentiment here expressed and the reservation drawn would have been as characteristic of Johnson as they were of Gladstone. But to die of laughter—this, too, seems to me a great euthanasia; and I think that for Johnson to have died thus, that night in Fleet Street, would have been a grand ending to 'a life radically wretched.' Well, he was destined to outlive another decade; and, selfishly, who can wish such a life as his, or such a Life as Boswell's, one jot shorter?

Strange, when you come to think of it, that of all the countless folk who have lived before our time on this planet not one is known in history or in legend as having died of laughter. Strange, too, that not to one of all the characters in romance has such an end been allotted. Has it ever struck you what a chance Shakespeare missed when he was finishing the Second Part of King Henry the Fourth? Falstaff was not the man to stand cowed and bowed while the new young king lectured him and cast him off. Little by little, as Hal proceeded in that portentous allocution, the humour of the situation would have mastered old Sir John. His face, blank with surprise at first, would presently have glowed and widened, and his whole bulk have begun to quiver. Lest he should miss one word, he would have mastered himself. But the final words would have been the signal for release of all the roars pent up in him; the welkin would have rung; the roars, belike, would have gradually subsided in dreadful rumblings of more than utterable or conquerable mirth. Thus and thus only might his life have been rounded off with dramatic fitness, *secundum ipsius naturam*. He never should have been left to babble of green fields and die 'an it had been any christom child.'

Falstaff is a triumph of comedic creation because we are kept laughing equally at and with him. Nevertheless, if I had the choice of sitting with him at the Boar's Head or with Johnson at the Turk's, I shouldn't hesitate for an instant. The agility of Falstaff's mind gains much of its effect by contrast with the massiveness of his body; but in contrast with Johnson's equal agility is Johnson's moral as well as physical bulk. His sallies 'tell' the more startlingly because of the noble weight of character behind them: they are the better because he makes them. In Falstaff there isn't this final incongruity and element of surprise. Falstaff is but a sublimated sample of 'the funny man.' We cannot, therefore, laugh so greatly with him as with Johnson. (Nor even at him; because we are not tickled so much by the weak points of a character whose points are all weak ones; also because we have no reverence trying to impose restraint upon us.) Still, Falstaff has indubitably the power to convulse us. I don't mean we ever are convulsed in reading

Henry the Fourth. No printed page, alas, can thrill us to extremities of laughter. These are ours only if the mirthmaker be a living man whose jests we hear as they come fresh from his own lips. All I claim for Falstaff is that he would be able to convulse us if he were alive and accessible. Few, as I have said, are the humorists who can induce this state. To master and dissolve us, to give us the joy of being worn down and tired out with laughter, is a success to be won by no man save in virtue of a rare staying-power. Laughter becomes extreme only if it be consecutive. There must be no pauses for recovery. Touch-and-go humour, however happy, is not enough. The jester must be able to grapple his theme and hang on to it, twisting it this way and that, and making it yield magically all manner of strange and precious things, one after another, without pause. He must have invention keeping pace with utterance. He must be inexhaustible. Only so can he exhaust us.

I have a friend whom I would praise. There are many other of my friends to whom I am indebted for much laughter; but I do believe that if all of them sent in their bills to-morrow and all of them overcharged me not a little, the total of all those totals would be less appalling than that which looms in my own vague estimate of what I owe to Comus. Comus I call him here in observance of the line drawn between public and private virtue, and in full knowledge that he would of all men be the least glad to be quite personally thanked and laurelled in the market-place for the hours he has made memorable among his cronies. No one is so diffident as he, no one so self-postponing. Many people have met him again and again without faintly suspecting 'anything much' in him. Many of his acquaintances—friends, too—relatives, even—have lived and died in the belief that he was quite ordinary. Thus is he the more greatly valued by his cronies. Thus do we pride ourselves on possessing some curious right quality to which alone he is responsive. But it would seem that either this asset of ours or its effect on him is intermittent. He can be dull and null enough with us sometimes—a mere asker of questions, or drawer of comparisons between this and that brand of cigarettes, or full expatiator on the merits of some new patent razor. A whole hour and more may be wasted in such humdrum and darkness. And then—something will have happened. There has come a spark in the murk; a flame now, presage of a radiance: Comus has begun. His face is a great part of his equipment. A cast of it might be somewhat akin to the comic mask of the ancients; but no cast could be worthy of it; mobility is the essence of it. It flickers and shifts in accord to the matter of his discourse; it contracts and it expands; is there anything its elastic can't express? Comus would be eloquent even were he dumb. And he is mellifluous. His voice, while he develops an idea or conjures up a scene, takes on a peculiar richness and unction. If he be describing an actual scene, voice and face are adaptable to those of the actual persons therein. But it is not in such mimicry that he excels. As a reporter he has rivals. For the most part, he moves on a higher plane that of mere fact: he imagines, he creates, giving you not a person, but a type, a synthesis, and not what anywhere has been, but what anywhere might be—what, as one feels, for all the absurdity of it, just would be. He knows his world well, and nothing human is alien to him, but certain skeins of life have a special hold on him, and he on them. In his youth he wished to be a clergyman; and over the clergy of all grades and denominations his genius hovers and swoops and ranges with a special mastery. Lawyers he loves less; yet the legal mind seems to lie almost as wide-open to him as the sacerdotal; and the legal manner in all its phases he can unerringly burlesque. In the minds of journalists, diverse journalists, he is not less thoroughly at home, so that of the wild contingencies imagined by him there is none about which he cannot reel off an oral 'leader' or 'middle' in the likeliest style, and with as much ease as he can preach a High Church or Low Church sermon on it. Nor are his improvisations limited by prose. If a theme call for nobler treatment, he becomes an unflagging fountain of ludicrously adequate blank-verse. Or again, he may deliver himself in rhyme. There is no form of utterance that comes amiss to him for interpreting the human comedy, or for broadening the farce into which that comedy is turned by him. Nothing can stop him when once he is in the vein. No appeals move him. He goes from strength to strength while his audience is more and more piteously debilitated.

What a gift to have been endowed with! What a power to wield! And how often I have envied Comus! But this envy of him has never taken root in me. His mind laughs, doubtless, at his own conceptions; but not his body. And if you tell him something that you have been sure will convulse him you are likely to be rewarded with no more than a smile betokening that he sees the point. Incomparable laughter-giver, he is not much a laugher. He is vintner, not toper. I would therefore not change places with him. I am well content to have been his beneficiary during thirty years, and to be so for as many more as may be given us.

ABOUT THE AUTHOR

Sir Henry Maximilian Beerbohm (August 24, 1872 – May 20, 1956) was an English parodist and caricaturist.

He was born in London, England, the younger half-brother of actor and producer Sir Herbert Beerbohm Tree. He was educated at Charterhouse School and Merton College, Oxford. It was during this time that he became part of the Wilde set, although Beerbohm was regarded as incomparable to anyone else. It was at school that he began writing. His "In Praise of Cosmetics" appeared in the first edition of the The Yellow Book, Aubrey Beardsley being art editor at the time. Beerbohm toured the United States while a young man, as a press agent for his brother's theatrical company.

His first book, The Works of Max Beerbohm, was published in 1896. Having been interviewed by George Bernard Shaw himself, in 1898 he followed Shaw as drama critic for the Saturday Review, on whose staff he remained until 1910. From 1935 onwards, he was an occasional if popular radio broadcaster, talking on cars and carriages and music halls for the BBC. His wit is shown often enough in his caricatures but his letters contain a carefully blended humour—a gentle admonishing of the excesses of the day—whilst remaining firmly tongue in cheek. His lifelong friend Reginald Turner, who was also an aesthete and a somewhat witty companion, saved many of Max's letters.

Beerbohm's best known works are A Christmas Garland (1912), a parody of literary styles, and Seven Men (1919), which includes "Enoch Soames", the tale of a poet who makes a deal with the Devil to find out how posterity will remember him, is also well known. In 1911 he wrote Zuleika Dobson, his only novel. Other works include The Happy Hypocrite (1897).

Beerbohm married the actress Florence Kahn in 1910. He was knighted in 1939. He died in Rapallo, Italy aged 83. His ashes were interred in the crypt of St. Paul's Cathedral, London.

Choose from Thousands of 1stWorldLibrary Classics By

A. M. Barnard	Booth Tarkington	Edward Everett Hale
Ada Leverson	Boyd Cable	Edward J. O'Biren
Adolphus William Ward	Bram Stoker	Edward S. Ellis
Aesop	C. Collodi	Edwin L. Arnold
Agatha Christie	C. E. Orr	Eleanor Atkins
Alexander Aaronsohn	C. M. Ingleby	Eleanor Hallowell Abbott
Alexander Kielland	Carolyn Wells	Eliot Gregory
Alexandre Dumas	Catherine Parr Traill	Elizabeth Gaskell
Alfred Gatty	Charles A. Eastman	Elizabeth McCracken
Alfred Ollivant	Charles Amory Beach	Elizabeth Von Arnim
Alice Duer Miller	Charles Dickens	Ellem Key
Alice Turner Curtis	Charles Dudley Warner	Emerson Hough
Alice Dunbar	Charles Farrar Browne	Emilie F. Carlen
Allen Chapman	Charles Ives	Emily Bronte
Alleyne Ireland	Charles Kingsley	Emily Dickinson
Ambrose Bierce	Charles Klein	Enid Bagnold
Amelia E. Barr	Charles Hanson Towne	Enilor Macartney Lane
Amory H. Bradford	Charles Lathrop Pack	Erasmus W. Jones
Andrew Lang	Charles Romyn Dake	Ernie Howard Pie
Andrew McFarland Davis	Charles Whibley	Ethel May Dell
Andy Adams	Charles Willing Beale	Ethel Turner
Angela Brazil	Charlotte M. Braeme	Ethel Watts Mumford
Anna Alice Chapin	Charlotte M. Yonge	Eugene Sue
Anna Sewell	Charlotte Perkins Stetson	Eugenie Foa
Annie Besant	Clair W. Hayes	Eugene Wood
Annie Hamilton Donnell	Clarence Day Jr.	Eustace Hale Ball
Annie Payson Call	Clarence E. Mulford	Evelyn Everett-green
Annie Roe Carr	Clemence Housman	Everard Cotes
Annonaymous	Confucius	F. H. Cheley
Anton Chekhov	Coningsby Dawson	F. J. Cross
Archibald Lee Fletcher	Cornelis DeWitt Wilcox	F. Marion Crawford
Arnold Bennett	Cyril Burleigh	Fannie E. Newberry
Arthur C. Benson	D. H. Lawrence	Federick Austin Ogg
Arthur Conan Doyle	Daniel Defoe	Ferdinand Ossendowski
Arthur M. Winfield	David Garnett	Fergus Hume
Arthur Ransome	Dinah Craik	Florence A. Kilpatrick
Arthur Schnitzler	Don Carlos Janes	Fremont B. Deering
Arthur Train	Donald Keyhoe	Francis Bacon
Atticus	Dorothy Kilner	Francis Darwin
B.H. Baden-Powell	Dougan Clark	Frances Hodgson Burnett
B. M. Bower	Douglas Fairbanks	Frances Parkinson Keyes
B. C. Chatterjee	E. Nesbit	Frank Gee Patchin
Baroness Emmuska Orczy	E. P. Roe	Frank Harris
Baroness Orczy	E. Phillips Oppenheim	Frank Jewett Mather
Basil King	E. S. Brooks	Frank L. Packard
Bayard Taylor	Earl Barnes	Frank V. Webster
Ben Macomber	Edgar Rice Burroughs	Frederic Stewart Isham
Bertha Muzzy Bower	Edith Van Dyne	Frederick Trevor Hill
Bjornstjerne Bjornson	Edith Wharton	Frederick Winslow Taylor

Friedrich Kerst	Hayden Carruth	James Branch Cabell
Friedrich Nietzsche	Helent Hunt Jackson	James DeMille
Fyodor Dostoyevsky	Helen Nicolay	James Joyce
G.A. Henty	Hendrik Conscience	James Lane Allen
G.K. Chesterton	Hendy David Thoreau	James Lane Allen
Gabrielle E. Jackson	Henri Barbusse	James Oliver Curwood
Garrett P. Serviss	Henrik Ibsen	James Oppenheim
Gaston Leroux	Henry Adams	James Otis
George A. Warren	Henry Ford	James R. Driscoll
George Ade	Henry Frost	Jane Abbott
Geroge Bernard Shaw	Henry James	Jane Austen
George Cary Eggleston	Henry Jones Ford	Jane L. Stewart
George Durston	Henry Seton Merriman	Janet Aldridge
George Ebers	Henry W Longfellow	Jens Peter Jacobsen
George Eliot	Herbert A. Giles	Jerome K. Jerome
George Gissing	Herbert Carter	Jessie Graham Flower
George MacDonald	Herbert N. Casson	John Buchan
George Meredith	Herman Hesse	John Burroughs
George Orwell	Hildegard G. Frey	John Cournos
George Sylvester Viereck	Homer	John F. Kennedy
George Tucker	Honore De Balzac	John Gay
George W. Cable	Horace B. Day	John Glasworthy
George Wharton James	Horace Walpole	John Habberton
Gertrude Atherton	Horatio Alger Jr.	John Joy Bell
Gordon Casserly	Howard Pyle	John Kendrick Bangs
Grace E. King	Howard R. Garis	John Milton
Grace Gallatin	Hugh Lofting	John Philip Sousa
Grace Greenwood	Hugh Walpole	John Taintor Foote
Grant Allen	Humphry Ward	Jonas Lauritz Idemil Lie
Guillermo A. Sherwell	Ian Maclaren	Jonathan Swift
Gulielma Zollinger	Inez Haynes Gillmore	Joseph A. Altsheler
Gustav Flaubert	Irving Bacheller	Joseph Carey
H. A. Cody	Isabel Cecilia Williams	Joseph Conrad
H. B. Irving	Isabel Hornibrook	Joseph E. Badger Jr
H.C. Bailey	Israel Abrahams	Joseph Hergesheimer
H. G. Wells	Ivan Turgenev	Joseph Jacobs
H. H. Munro	J.G.Austin	Jules Vernes
H. Irving Hancock	J. Henri Fabre	Julian Hawthrone
H. R. Naylor	J. M. Barrie	Julie A Lippmann
H. Rider Haggard	J. M. Walsh	Justin Huntly McCarthy
H. W. C. Davis	J. Macdonald Oxley	Kakuzo Okakura
Haldeman Julius	J. R. Miller	Karle Wilson Baker
Hall Caine	J. S. Fletcher	Kate Chopin
Hamilton Wright Mabie	J. S. Knowles	Kenneth Grahame
Hans Christian Andersen	J. Storer Clouston	Kenneth McGaffey
Harold Avery	J. W. Duffield	Kate Langley Bosher
Harold McGrath	Jack London	Kate Langley Bosher
Harriet Beecher Stowe	Jacob Abbott	Katherine Cecil Thurston
Harry Castlemon	James Allen	Katherine Stokes
Harry Coghill	James Andrews	L. A. Abbot
Harry Houidini	James Baldwin	L. T. Meade

L. Frank Baum	Paul G. Tomlinson	T. S. Arthur
Latta Griswold	Paul Severing	The Princess Der Ling
Laura Dent Crane	Percy Brebner	Thomas A. Janvier
Laura Lee Hope	Percy Keese Fitzhugh	Thomas A Kempis
Laurence Housman	Peter B. Kyne	Thomas Anderton
Lawrence Beasley	Plato	Thomas Bailey Aldrich
Leo Tolstoy	Quincy Allen	Thomas Bulfinch
Leonid Andreyev	R. Derby Holmes	Thomas De Quincey
Lewis Carroll	R. L. Stevenson	Thomas Dixon
Lewis Sperry Chafer	R. S. Ball	Thomas H. Huxley
Lilian Bell	Rabindranath Tagore	Thomas Hardy
Lloyd Osbourne	Rahul Alvares	Thomas More
Louis Hughes	Ralph Bonehill	Thornton W. Burgess
Louis Joseph Vance	Ralph Henry Barbour	U. S. Grant
Louis Tracy	Ralph Victor	Upton Sinclair
Louisa May Alcott	Ralph Waldo Emmerson	Valentine Williams
Lucy Fitch Perkins	Rene Descartes	Various Authors
Lucy Maud Montgomery	Ray Cummings	Vaughan Kester
Luther Benson	Rex Beach	Victor Appleton
Lydia Miller Middleton	Rex E. Beach	Victor G. Durham
Lyndon Orr	Richard Harding Davis	Victoria Cross
M. Corvus	Richard Jefferies	Virginia Woolf
M. H. Adams	Richard Le Gallienne	Wadsworth Camp
Margaret E. Sangster	Robert Barr	Walter Camp
Margret Howth	Robert Frost	Walter Scott
Margaret Vandercook	Robert Gordon Anderson	Washington Irving
Margaret W. Hungerford	Robert L. Drake	Wilbur Lawton
Margret Penrose	Robert Lansing	Wilkie Collins
Maria Edgeworth	Robert Lynd	Willa Cather
Maria Thompson Daviess	Robert Michael Ballantyne	Willard F. Baker
Mariano Azuela	Robert W. Chambers	William Dean Howells
Marion Polk Angellotti	Rosa Nouchette Carey	William le Queux
Mark Overton	Rudyard Kipling	W. Makepeace Thackeray
Mark Twain	Saint Augustine	William W. Walter
Mary Austin	Samuel B. Allison	William Shakespeare
Mary Catherine Crowley	Samuel Hopkins Adams	Winston Churchill
Mary Cole	Sarah Bernhardt	Yei Theodora Ozaki
Mary Hastings Bradley	Sarah C. Hallowell	Yogi Ramacharaka
Mary Roberts Rinehart	Selma Lagerlof	Young E. Allison
Mary Rowlandson	Sherwood Anderson	Zane Grey
M. Wollstonecraft Shelley	Sigmund Freud	
Maud Lindsay	Standish O'Grady	
Max Beerbohm	Stanley Weyman	
Myra Kelly	Stella Benson	
Nathaniel Hawthrone	Stella M. Francis	
Nicolo Machiavelli	Stephen Crane	
O. F. Walton	Stewart Edward White	
Oscar Wilde	Stijn Streuvels	
Owen Johnson	Swami Abhedananda	
P.G. Wodehouse	Swami Parmananda	
Paul and Mabel Thorne	T. S. Ackland	